LIFE AFTEI

THE DR. PINKY MILLER STORY

BY DR. PINKY MILLER

LIFE AFTER LEAN ON ME: THE DR. PINKY MILLER STORY

Published by Know Our Story, LLC
3035 Stone Mountain Street #2233
Lithonia, GA 30058

Printed in the United States of America

ISBN-13:978-1-497-48227-2
ISBN-10: 1497482275

Cover photo, hair and make-up by Octavia Wilson

Library of Congress Control Number: 2014906165

Eastside High School logo and photos used with permission from Paterson Public Schools.

Warner Bros. is the owner of *Lean on Me*. *Life after Lean on Me* is not authorized by or affiliated with Warner Bros.

All Scripture quotations, unless otherwise indicated, are taken from the *Holy Bible, New International Version®. NIV®.* Copyright © 1973, 1978, 1984 by International Bible Society. Used by permission of Zondervan. All rights reserved.

DISCLAIMER AND/OR LEGAL NOTICES

www.Know-Our-Story.com

A Word of Warning

Among other themes, this autobiography spotlights multiple forms of child abuse, the deleterious effect of abuse on childhood education, the psychology of victimhood, its persistent—and often camouflaged—echoes throughout adult life, and the slow healing that can finally begin under the care, stability, and safety of even one dedicated parent, trustworthy adult, or mental health professional.

Though several incidents of abuse present in early drafts of this book have been removed to maintain contiguous thematic focus and readability of the material, various scenes remain graphic, and reader discretion is advised.

Names and relations of individuals have been changed to protect identities.

Books in the *Life after Lean on Me* Biographical Series

Life after Lean on Me: The Dr. Pinky Miller Story

Life after Lean on Me: The Dissertation Research. What happened to the REAL students after the movie Lean on Me?

Life after Lean on Me: The Diana Moore Story (coming soon)

Life after Lean on Me: The Jason Booker Story (coming soon)

Life after Lean on Me: The Dr. Pinky Miller Story II (coming soon)

www.know-our-story.com

CONTENTS

Even where there is no hope,
one person still can change the world
and inspire others to stand up and do the same.

DEDICATION

My mother is my SHERO in life and in my book.
I love YOU Mommy!!!

1 GANGS AND GHOSTS

PATERSON, NEW JERSEY—1982

(Photos Courtesy of Dr. Pinky Miller)

Shortly before I started my freshman year at notorious Eastside High School, a student knifed a teacher.

Eastside's student body ran the gamut, from those who were violent drug dealers and gang members, to those who wanted to learn. Many Eastside students were bullied, beaten, raped, and had their popular clothing, sneakers, and jewelry stolen. Teachers dated students, and students had babies by teachers and administrators.

I had three female cousins who lived with me and my two brothers who all attended Eastside. Some relatives became pregnant and dropped out, while others graduated.

(Lonnie Seldon - Brother)   (Brent Keys - Brother)

Many instructors, afraid of the violent students, were not able to teach.

Outside the school, drug dealers, drug addicts, gang members, alcoholics, and prostitutes circled the community. Students were forced to wade through these hazards every day as they traveled to and from school.

Stories of Eastside often appeared in the newspapers and on television news broadcasts.

I didn't get to choose which high school I would attend. I had to go to Eastside.

My best friend Jackie—my "Puerto Rican Soul Sista"; I was her "Black Soul Sista"—arrived in front of my house, preparing to walk to Eastside together for our first day as freshmen. I stood up from my porch, which was actually nothing more than five concrete steps, and gave her a "let's suck it up and make the best of it" smile.

I was used to sucking it up. My cousin often teased me brutally while my mother was away working, for not knowing who my father was. She would say to me, "Where is your long lost father?" I thought I was an accident. A mistake. My mother, a single parent of six, including three female cousins worked two full-time jobs. She wasn't home often.

Jackie's smile trembled. "Pinky? Are you ready for this?"

"No, I'm scared! I even cried last night. I do not want to go to Eastside!" Across the street sat the elementary school we had happily gone to and the swing set we had played on all our lives. Younger kids merrily entered its doors without us.

We started the seven-block walk toward high school.

Jackie said, "At least you and I will be there for each other, though I wish all my older brothers, sister, and cousins were our age instead so they'd be going with us. Did your brother or cousins tell you about all the gangs there are?"

"Yeah. Street cliques and gangs, and some "religious" oriented cliques and gangs. Others are racial groups—African American, Hispanic, Puerto Rican, Dominican, Jamaican. . . .," I responded, thinking about who would be the kindest to us and who I (we) should steer clear of.

"There are also the Five-Percenters. I heard they're considered an offshoot of the Nation of Islam. They wear crocheted hats called kufis."

So many gangs. Silently I asked God to keep us safe. Never had I been so terrified.

"Jackie, remember when my cousin Olivia got into a fight with another student by Eastside? Actually, it happened right across the street from the school on the Market Street side, the back of the school. That fight got big so fast." It probably wasn't the best thing to be thinking about, but I couldn't help it. "The other girl had family who joined in, then some of my family joined in. Something small erupted into something really big! Family was fighting against family! It went from sticks to baseball bats to guns drawn."

"I remember the fighting moved all the way to your house," Jackie recalled.

"I had family members fighting right in front of my house. It was awful! Thank God the police arrived to end it, and no one was hurt bad. That gave me such bad feelings about attending Eastside. I do not want to go to this school!"

Several groups of kids walked in the same direction we did, some ahead of us, some behind us. I was thankful that though my family was poor, we were middle class compared to a lot of other poverty-stricken families in Paterson. We lived in a home rather than in an apartment building or the projects.

At the corners we paused for traffic, then we crossed streets that were increasingly littered with trash and crack vials. The ghetto. "Da hood." More high school kids appeared and walked toward the school. Dozens of them. Hundreds. More than three thousand students attended Eastside.

Jackie and I approached the school on the Market Street side. The other main entrance was on Park Avenue, where a lot of African American drug dealers and users hung out. The Market Street side was the domain of the Dominicans, Hispanics, and Latinos.

As terrified little freshmen, we walked past a battered chain-link fence and rectangles of ill-tended brown grass toward the hulking monstrosity of a school.

(Photo Courtesy of Pinky Miller)

Eastside was three stories of dirty brick and dirty glass, speckled with graffiti as high as spray cans could spew. The building looked like an abandoned factory, or a prison, except for the big metal doors through which kids streamed daily. The doors had long ago been painted orange and blue—the team colors of the Mighty Ghosts. "Ghosts" because the school had been built atop the site of an old cemetery.

(Photos created by Salvatore Scarpinato, English Teacher - Photos Courtesy of EHS Yearbook, 1986)

Now the orange and blue paint was chipped, peeled, and graffitied.

Jackie and I walked in through the doors with the droves of other students. Not knowing what to do or where to go, we moved with them up the stairs.

Near us a voice like a drill sergeant's boomed over the ruckus, but I couldn't see where the voice originated. I was even more scared now. Hearing the voice and not seeing anyone attached to it seemed crazy.

"Jackie, what *is* that?! Where is that voice coming from?" I had to raise my own voice so she could hear me.

"The intercom system?"

"I don't think so. It doesn't sound right."

The voice kept getting louder. It came closer and closer.

A tall, slender man in a professional-looking brown suit appeared, a bullhorn held to his mouth. He bellowed, "Walk to the right! Walk to the right!"

Why was he yelling at us?

"Walk to the right! My name is Joe Clark and I am your new principal! Things have changed; the old Eastside is gone. Welcome to the new Eastside!"

We moved forward like fish guided by the sea's current.

"Students, proceed to the auditorium," he ordered through the bullhorn, almost directly in our faces.

I asked him, "Where is the auditorium?"

(Photo Courtesy of EHS Yearbook, 1984)

(Photo Courtesy of EHS Yearbook, 1986)

"Walk to the right!"

We practically dove to the right and scampered past him.

He kept repeating himself and continued to stride down the dingy, graffiti-sprayed hallway. "Walk to the right!"

Teachers stood in the middle of the hallway like dots of a yellow line painted down the center of a road. They told the students to stay to the right and keep moving toward the auditorium.

(Mr. Korenda, science teacher - holding his "Keep Right" sign - Photo Courtesy of EHS Yearbook, 1987)

We didn't know where the auditorium was. We were lost little freshmen. So we simply followed the crowd. Upperclassmen stood in groups, smirking and cracking on the newbies. "Look at the scared little freshies!"

Finally we reached the auditorium.

It was massive. Two to three stories high, wider than it was tall, a broad stage across the far end with a microphone stand near the center, more chairs than I'd ever seen, and enough air space for a helicopter to maneuver. Everyone streamed inside then waved and called out greetings as we saw friends we knew from elementary school. Teachers told everyone to find a seat and to be quiet. There was too much excitement to be quiet, but we went and sat down.

As I looked around, my fear evaporated. This place was amazing to me. I saw several people I knew from School Number 24, but there were many more students I didn't know. I was actually excited.

Jackie elbowed me. "Pinky! Look, there's a few of our girlfriends!"

If you're wondering why "Pinky," when I was born I looked like a little white baby, and every time I would cry or get angry, my skin color would turn red. My mother didn't want to call me "Reddy," but she and my Aunt Myra came up with "Pinky." The nickname stuck, and it fit. I loved—and *always* wore—pink.

When all the students had entered the auditorium, Mr. Clark strode onto the stage, bold as a burst of lightning. He set the bullhorn down and took command of the microphone.

Several moments passed before he quieted the students and got them settled.

Then he said, "*I* am your new principal, Mr. Clark! And *you* are here to learn! You are here to get an education! Things that happened here before are not going to happen anymore! There will be no fighting! If you fight, you will be suspended for ten days! You will also get suspended if you do not follow the rules! You will wear ID badges. If you come to school without your ID badge, you will not be allowed to enter! You will not be late for class! This is the *new* Eastside High School!"

The students in the auditorium stared at him, most of them silent. This man did not play.

Awestruck, I glanced at Jackie beside me. Her amazed expression echoed what I was thinking: *This is so great! Eastside is going to be so much better than I expected!*

Behind us a couple of kids mumbled, "Whatever." "Who does he think he is?"

I thought, *He's the man who's going to make sure we're safe at this school!*

For another ten minutes, Mr. Clark laid down the law and told us the rules, regulations, and policies.

Then he said, "Every last one of you is going to learn the alma mater—the school song! When asked to, you will recite it, you will sing it, and you will know it in both English and Spanish! You will have pride in your school and pride in yourselves!

"You were born with two strikes against you: being poor, and being black or another minority! Don't strike out! Get your education! Your education is your homerun out of the ghetto! Whatever circumstances you were born into do not dictate how far you can go in life! They do not dictate your future!"

"If you have a problem, you can come and talk to me between six and eight in the morning, or you can talk to me after school."

Wow, was he serious? We could just go and talk to him as early as six in the morning if we had a problem? We couldn't even do that in elementary school!

Students around me sat in stunned disbelief. I heard someone murmur my own thought in amazement. "Is he serious?"

"Now I'm going to introduce your teachers then send you to your homerooms!"

When Mr. Clark had finished speaking, we all began to find our way to our homerooms.

In the hallways, Mr. Clark was a leading subject of student discussions.

Like him or not, he was a hard man to ignore.

As the semester got underway, I became acquainted with the school rules, teachers, and other students as well as Mr. Clark.

Mr. Clark called us by name, often using the bullhorn. "Pinky! How are you doing?"

"Fine. I—"

"Good! Glad to hear it! Everyone, walk to the right!"

(Photos Courtesy of EHS Yearbook, 1985)

He and his bullhorn were always visible in one of the hallways between classes, but we saw Mr. Clark most often in the cafeteria, keeping a close eye on the students. Before he arrived at Eastside, food fights dominated the lunch hours.

During lunchtime around the third week of school, his bullhorn made me jump.

"Pinky! Come over here and bring your friends with you!" Since all students had to wear their ID badges, I wore mine, but he didn't need it to know my name. I always wore pink! We hurried over to him. "You five are going to sing the alma mater."

He held up the bullhorn in front of us, and we sang it.

> Fair Eastside, by thy side we'll stand
> and always praise thy name,
> and ever lend our hearts and hands to help increase thy fame.
> The honor of old Eastside High brings forth our loyalty.
> So cheer for dear old Eastside High! Lead on to victory!

After we finished, he said, "Thank you. How are you girls doing in school? How are your classes going?"

"Good."

"Fine, glad to hear it. Go sit down and eat."

If we ever had a problem or wanted to talk to him for a minute, he'd listen to us while his eyes scanned the room. Because he frequented the cafeteria, and because he listened to our questions or concerns, the students knew that they mattered to him.

One of my best friends from elementary school, Cecelia, had always been shy. The day she introduced me to her relative in Eastside's cafeteria, however, I doubted they could be genetically linked.

"Pinky, I see my cousin coming over here. You've never met him. Pinky, this is—"

A boy plunked down right beside me and playfully tugged my hair. "—Benny. How do you do, Pinky? You're pleased to meet me!" He grinned with a complete lack of self-consciousness.

I transitioned a threatening smile into an eye roll. "Get away from me! Cecelia, would you please get your cousin?" But on the inside, I was delighted. What a rascal.

He moved closer and lightly jabbed his elbow into my side.

"*Cecelia!*" I said in mock exasperation. "Come get your cousin!"

Other males had touched me in bad ways. Benny wasn't touching me that way at all. He was sitting close, yet I didn't move away.

We talked for the rest of the lunch hour—well, mostly Benny talked, but he included us—and he sat with us during lunch several days in a row. He always elbowed me or tugged my hair, and he always sat close. Day by day he sat even closer.

Still I didn't put distance between us.

One day he said, "Pinky, you're going to be my girlfriend."

"No, I am not going to be your girlfriend!" I couldn't help smiling anymore.

"Yes, you are."

"Nope."

"Yep."

A couple of weeks later, Benny started walking me home from school. I became his girlfriend.

Mr. Clark started each morning by giving students "the word of the day"—a new vocabulary word—over the school's intercom. When we went to our classes, that day's word and its definition were written on the chalkboards. Throughout each day, Mr. Clark stopped students in the hallways and asked them the word of the day and its meaning. Occasionally he told them to use the word in a sentence.

Some students would duck and hide from him, trying not to be called out to sing the alma mater or if they didn't know the word for the day.

One day, my friend Diana had the misfortune of not ducking far enough.

"Diana!" Mr. Clark's bullhorn exclaimed. "How are you? How is your mother?"

"She's better, thank—"

"Good! Glad to hear it. What's the word of the day?"

"Uh . . ."

"Expeditiously!" he said.

Diana hesitated. "What do you mean?"

Mr. Clark said, "Go to class real fast!"

"Okay." She turned around to go to class.

"Diana, come back here," he said.

She went and stood in front of him.

"That's what the word means. *Expeditiously* means to move fast."

"Okay."

Then he said, "Now go to class expeditiously!"

And she did.

"Hi, Pinky!" Mr. Clark said.

"Hi, Mr. Clark."

"Tell me the word of the day."

"Expeditiously."

"What does it mean?"

Oh really, Mr. Clark! I grinned. "It means to move fast."

"Good. Everyone, keep it moving! You have to *want* to get an education in order to get out of the ghetto!"

I followed Diana to class.

Mr. Clark started to have the school interior cleaned up. As part of that effort, the maintenance guys smoothed fresh coats of paint over the graffiti on the walls and doors. When students added new graffiti to the walls, Mr. Clark held those students accountable. As soon as new graffiti went up, the student was made to work with the maintenance guys to paint over it.

That proved to be an effective deterrent, but it didn't end the defacement.

So Mr. Clark gathered up the graffiti artists. He said, "If you're going to paint on the walls, I'm going to let you! But instead of painting something ugly, I want you create something that looks good, something that's much more thought-provoking! Something that will instill pride in Eastside High School!"

Beautiful murals began to appear. A lot of students who had put up graffiti turned into artists who added color and spirit to the many corridors of Eastside.

Mr. Clark's relationship with teachers depended upon who the teacher was and if the teacher bought in to his philosophy, care, and concern for the staff and students. Some teachers he treated very well. Some teachers, in my opinion, he treated with significant disrespect. The teachers who bought into his way of running the school didn't have any problems with him. The teachers who didn't agree with him were fired, forced out, or thrown out.

It may have been very hard for some of the teachers who taught at Eastside prior to Mr. Clark's arrival. People tend to be afraid of change, especially when they don't understand what is going on. Mr. Clark did not always share his vision with the teachers, and that made it difficult for some of them.

At times people simply have to trust a new leader. New leaders are commonly looked upon as if they don't know what they're doing because they're new to the position. Mr. Clark may have been new to the position of principal at Eastside High School, but his dogmatic leadership style and reputation were very well known, since he had worked as principal at Public School Number 6 for several years.

I believe Mr. Clark respected the teachers who were doing their jobs. Many students felt as though there were some teachers who just didn't care whether they learned anything or not. When Mr. Clark asked the students their opinions of the teachers, we shared our opinion with him honestly. And if there was a cause for concern, he would deal with that teacher immediately. Sometimes he would discipline teachers or administrators in front of the students.

The job that Mr. Clark had, could not be faked. You could tell he was to be in it *100 percent* committed.

Eastside was in major disarray, and only with support from Dr. Frank Napier, the superintendent, and the Paterson community did Mr. Clark bring change to Eastside High School. He had help and support from the community, especially from the community's churches and ministries.

I believe Mr. Clark was a good principal and leader and that he used effective strategies to change the high school for the better. He focused on order and structure.

He implemented a plan to keep the drugs and drug dealers out of EHS. Specifically, Mr. Clark replaced door locks and old fences, he replaced security guards he deemed ineffective, and he kept watch on the students he perceived most likely to open the door and let the drug pushers in.

Mr. Clark stationed security guards outside the school near the entrance fences, even though some teachers were fearful because they felt the school would be "guard-less" inside. However, Mr. Clark instituted a plan for teachers and administrators to serve as in-school security. Teachers stood in the corridors before and between class periods. In addition, the administrators roved along the corridors until students were settled in their classrooms.

Mr. Clark initiated the identification card system and rigorously enforced it. Every student, teacher, and staff member had to wear a color-coded picture ID badge that was checked by security guards upon entering the building. The badge had to be worn and visible at all times. Anyone who did not have their ID was not allowed to enter the school or had to pay a fine to receive another one.

He had his controversies, too. Once, he threw a bunch of students out of the school—students he thought were just hanging around, selling drugs, fighting, and causing all kinds of trouble. I didn't mind him kicking them out. They scared me simply by being there, and, believe it or not, that constant fear stopped me from learning.

A number of community members and Paterson Board of Education members thought some of Mr. Clark's strategies for his students—namely, discipline and fear—and his leadership style were too inflexible. However, viewing at it as a student who was there during those turbulent times, I saw his strategies as protective of us students who wanted to learn, from other students who did not want to learn.

Mr. Clark had to deal with students who not only didn't want to learn, but they also wanted to sell drugs and inflict pain on other students. Had he used any other strategies and tactics, I don't think Mr. Clark would have been able to reach as many students as he did.

As his students, most of us looked up to Mr. Clark and appreciated what he did for us. To us, Mr. Clark was phenomenal.

He was phenomenal to watch, and he always had a strong hand and a strong, loud mouth with that bullhorn, but he was also friendly, and caring, and made us feel that we were important to him. He became the father that many of us never had. I frequently thanked God for him.

Gradually, Eastside became a safe haven for me. I actually found myself wanting to be more at school than at home. Eastside was a pleasure. Home life was turbulent.

***

After the Mighty Ghosts won the basketball game, we all sang the alma mater. Mr. Clark made us sing it after every game, win or lose.

FAIR EASTSIDE

(Mr. Clark & students singing the alma mater at a football game - Photos Courtesy of EHS Yearbook, 1989)

Then, along with the other JV cheerleaders, I grabbed my pompoms and followed our team out of the gymnasium.

A few paces in front of me, the captain of the basketball team bent close to the captain of the cheerleading squad and softly kissed her. Taking her hand, he walked with her among our teammates into the hallway.

He was handsome. And they looked sweet and beautiful and perfect.

Raw pain knifed through my heart, and dreadful memories began to surface.

In my experience, a male's attention toward a girl wasn't often nice. . .

2 BEGINNINGS

Our two-story house had an attic . . . and a basement. On the second floor, I used to share a small bedroom with two of my older cousins. My bed had been against the wall with its foot next to the hall entry door.

Dark, dank basements can be scary to any child. When I was very young, only five years old, our basement became much worse.

My cousin Andrew, older than me by ten or eleven years, lived with us from time to time after his mother, Aunt Henrietta, passed away. He slept in our attic. He was constantly in trouble for stealing, sometimes stealing cars, so the rest of the time he was in juvenile detention centers.

He was my favorite cousin, my favorite cousin, my favorite cousin. I keep repeating that because once upon a time, he was my favorite cousin Andrew, who would always show me a lot of attention, give me candy, hug me a lot, play with me, touch me, and we would spend afternoons and Saturday mornings together watching cartoons (I loved watching the *Flintstones*).

One night, I slowly awoke to a big hand rubbing my back.

"Be quiet. Shh," Andrew whispered near my head.

He pulled back my covers, picked me up, and carried me down two flights of stairs to the grimy basement where we sometimes played.

He closed the door behind us.

My cousin stood me on the floor and touched me all over my body where no one had ever touched me before.

It felt confusing. I didn't know why he was doing this.

Then he undressed my bottom half, and pulled my panties down.

He laid me face down in a pile of dirty clothes then pulled his pants down and lay on top of me. Pressing something hard onto my backside, he rubbed up and down on my backside with that something hard. It hurt. It hurt a lot.

I was scared and did not understand what was happening to me. I stared at the white washing machine and dryer with tears rolling down my face. I did not know what he was doing, but I knew what he was doing was not good.

When he finished (ejaculation), he took me to my bedroom and put me back in my bed. As I lay there, he went upstairs to the attic where he slept. I cried silently in my bed, unable to sleep until almost morning.

The next day, he acted as if things were normal.

I thought, *why did he hurt me? What was it that he did? There was the pressure of his body on top of me and pain that I felt on my bottom.*

How could he do that to me, his favorite cousin?

The dark nights in the basement happened often.

Little by little, I began to understand that he was manipulating me with the candy and attention, and that when he hurt me at night in the basement, it was wrong.

How could he do that to me? His favorite cousin.

Andrew was my favorite cousin.

I didn't tell.

***

I participated in the brand-new federally funded head start program in the early 70s. I attended Daycare 100 located in

Paterson where my mother served as an assistant head start teacher. I began to learn how to read and write when I was about three or four years old. I had a very good memory.

During the end of the school year/closing ceremonies, I was asked to memorize and recite a poem for the assembly of more than 100 students, teachers, and administrators.

There were so many people there. I remember my name being called, and as I began walking up to the stage, I was a little nervous, but I felt very happy to be able to stand on the stage and recite this poem that my mother taught me.

I still remember that poem 46 years later and now that I'm older, I wonder… What were they thinking? Why this poem? Was this poem appropriate? What was going on during that time? Why is this poem significant enough to be recited at the closing ceremony of the head start program?

The Poem - This Old Heart of Mine
This old heart of mine; got me drinking wine.
Smoking reefers too; even sniffing glue.
I tried hard to stop; while drinking soda pop; my mother called
the cops;
And they ran after me; I ran up a tree; smoking in LSD, and
that was the end of me
Dee, dee, dee, dee dee, dee.

When I finished saying the poem, the audience cheered and clapped loudly I was happy, my mother was happy. I returned to my seat smiling with glee. As a child, it was just a poem. As an adult, the words have more meaning to me.

The question remains in my mind, what were they thinking? Teaching a four year old child this poem? I assume that they were trying to teach the very simple and significant lesson to not use drugs. Maybe that poem stuck in my head ever since I was a little girl because I have never smoked reefers (marijuana) or used any other illegal drugs and I am very proud of that! It worked for me! Or could it have been the experiences of me seeing some of my family members addicted to and using drugs?

When I was a little girl, I used to be a tattletale. I would tell on everybody and I would tell everything. So my siblings had to be very careful about what they did around me because I frequently told on them. I had a very keen sense of smell. My nose and I could tell when someone was smoking marijuana. I knew the smell, and I would say "Ooooohhhhh somebody is smoking reefers" and I would tell my mother.

I remember being called "little reefer" because I told on everyone. I am not exactly sure how my nose became so keen to the smell of marijuana. I can only assume that someone in my family or people who were close to my family were smoking marijuana on a regular basis around me.

My official school days began at Public School Number 24, right across the street from my house.

When I first entered the building as a scared little kindergartener not knowing who these teachers or children were, kindhearted Miss Weiler (Volpe) had her arms open for me and gave me a big hug. I melted right there. I fell in love with school and Miss Weiler on the spot!

She did the same with every child who entered her kindergarten class. We didn't know who each other was or what all the things in the classroom were, but we all thought Miss Weiler was wonderful.

After the first week, somehow I managed to be late for school every day. I think because my older siblings, cousins, and I lived so close to school we thought we had plenty of time, and we *had* to finish watching the *Flintstones* cartoon every morning! Who could turn off the *Flintstones*?

As we hurried across the street, we sang, "Flintstones! Meet the Flintstones! Have a yabba-dabba-doo time, a dabba-doo time!"

School started at 8:35, and I arrived at 8:50 (sharp!), which made me late for school.

I loved my kindergarten teacher, Miss Weiler tremendously, and she loved me, despite my fashionably late arrivals singing the "Flintstones."

When my mother was home, she was often stressed, short-tempered, and could swear a sailor into silence (and still can). Though my mother wasn't one for giving hugs, Miss Weiler was. She gave each of us a hug when we walked in every morning. Sometimes when no one was around, she gave me extra hugs. Miss Weiler always spoke with warmth and instructed with encouragement.

"Very nice pictures, everyone," she'd say. "Very nice work. Tomorrow we'll work on coloring inside the lines even better. And Olandha,"—for a while she called me by my birth name—"maybe you'll like to try a crayon color other than a shade of pink? Now everyone, come pick out a sticker."

When we did especially well on our schoolwork, Miss Weiler let us go out to the playground early and stay outside longer. A few times when we did our best work, she took us to get ice cream cones.

She was available to me and the other children, and she made us feel special, often just by listening with her bright eyes and big smile. I wanted to do my best work so that I would never disappoint her. I wanted to do my work well to make her happy. Her being happy kept school fun.

At the end of the day, I didn't want to go home. I wanted to stay at school.

When it was time for me to go on to first grade, I was sad that I would have to leave her behind. On one of the last days of kindergarten, Miss Weiler secretly told me that she loved me so much that she wanted to go to first grade with me, and then she did. That really made me feel special, and I needed that.

So I had the same teacher for kindergarten and first grade. Even after first grade, she continued to keep a close eye on me and give me hugs. She knew that I'd liked to read ever since I had been in the Head Start program and learned to read when I was four, and encouraged me to read and learn as much as I could.

Miss Weiler was the best first teacher I could have had.

At home, my Siamese cat, India, protected me. If someone moved too fast near us or bothered me, she tried to scratch them. I often wanted India to scratch my cousin Andrew when I thought about him hurting me, and sometimes she did.

India was my best friend. I spent a lot of fun times holding her, talking to her, and taking care of her.

One day my mother brought home another Siamese cat, a male cat named "12-50," because that's how much she paid for him— $12.50. 12-50 and India had kittens. I watched her give birth to them, and that was an amazing thing. My mother told me I couldn't touch the kittens until India allowed me to, because some mother cats killed their kittens when human scent was on the babies instead of theirs.

When they grew we couldn't keep all the cats, so my mother gave most of them away. Then we were back down to two cats.

We kept India, and that was good enough for me.

I loved India, and she gave me a little of the protection I wished I could have from my mother.

More than ever before, I wanted to be closer to my mother. I started to cling to her. I wanted more of her attention. Often when we sat on the couch and watched television, I tried to burrow against her.

Sometimes her arm lightly pushed me away, and I didn't understand why. Maybe she was tired. Maybe she didn't know how to love me. Maybe I was too much for her to handle then. Maybe I was becoming too needy as a child.

I only knew that I continually wanted to snuggle up against my mother. I missed her because she was always working.

Even before first grade, I frequently had severe nosebleeds. My nose would bleed if I became too hot, if I became too cold, if I blew my nose too hard, or my nose would bleed just because.

My godmother, a very good friend of my mother's with an even bigger heart, lived on 12th Avenue in Paterson. She had thirteen children and still basically adopted me as one of her own. My mother often took me to my godmother's house. I spent a lot of time there, and every few weeks I stayed the night.

My godmother was from the south and had an old folk's remedy that stopped nosebleeds. She'd tie a cold set of keys onto a long string, hold me close to her, and, gripping only the string, rest the keys on my back. The coldness from the keys would stop my nose from bleeding.

One day my godmother's nephews, Martin, who lived with her told his aunt that he'd lend a hand to stop my nose from bleeding. He took me into his bedroom, sat me on his lap, and laid the keys on my back.

Then he began rubbing up against my bottom with something hard, over and over again.

He held me down firmly and grinded on my bottom, while I tried to keep tissues pressed to my bleeding nose and he held the keys on my back.

I didn't understand what was happening or what he was doing. I thought he was trying to help, but it felt wrong, bad, and my nose was bleeding into a saturated hanky.

I didn't tell.

This was the first time he had ever done this. It wasn't the last. I longed to be close to my mother.

***

When I was six, my thirty-year-old cousin from New York, Nicholas, came to live with us for a while. He slept in the living room on the pullout couch.

Early every Saturday morning I rushed downstairs in my pajamas to watch cartoons before anyone else could wake up and come change the channel. Nicholas watched cartoons with me—the *Flintstones*, *Magilla Gorilla*, *Tom and Jerry*, and others.

One morning, rather than fold up the bed back into a couch, Nicholas told me I could sit on the bed with him. I sat on the corner near the TV.

When the commercials came on, he began to tickle me. As he did, he moved me from the corner of the bed and pulled me onto his lap as he lay in the bed. The cartoon came back on, and he stopped tickling me. I sat on his lap and watched TV.

During commercials, Nicholas continued playing with me and tickling me as I lay back on top of him and laughed. Then he pulled me up and sat me on his stomach, and tickled me as I laughed and giggled from the horseplay. Suddenly his thing popped out of his pajama pants. It (his penis) was standing straight up.

He said, "Whoops, it slipped out. Do you want to touch it?"

I said "no!" and I jumped off the bed, ran upstairs to my bedroom with my heart pounding, and waited for everyone else to wake up.

I stared at my closed bedroom door. Nicholas was older than me, bigger, and I didn't know him well. He had tickled me, but now I was afraid of him.

Why did family and friends keep doing this? What was happening? Did Nicholas want to hurt me?

I didn't tell.

***

I wondered why my mother let everybody and anybody live with us, and why she even let these bad people come near us. And

I wondered why so many older boys and men in my family touched me like Cousin Andrew did.

Some people in our family behaved strangely in others ways.

After I walked home from school one afternoon, I had to go the bathroom really bad. An uncle who also lived with us was in the one bathroom that we all had to share.

I knocked on the door, but he wouldn't open it. I knocked again and said, "I have to go to the bathroom!"

"I'm using the bathroom!" he growled. "Go away!"

I walked away but came back five minutes later and knocked again. I really *really* needed to go now. I kept knocking on the door and said, "I gotta pee! Open the door!"

My uncle hollered, "Go away!"

"Open the door!"

My uncle would not open the door.

Earlier in the year, my brother had nailed a small hole in the bathroom door, and we kids could peek in on the person using the bathroom. My brother had gotten a beating for that, and my mother had stopped up the hole with a tiny piece of tissue.

Ever since birth, inquisitiveness had been my constant companion. I pulled the tissue out of the hole then peeked into the bathroom to see what my uncle was doing. He was not using the bathroom. He was giving himself a needle, and he had some plastic blue thing wrapped around his arm.

Was he sick? Why didn't he go to the doctor to get his shots? I was mad now. "Uncle, I see you! You not using the bathroom! I'm telling mommy!"

"Get out of here," he growled.

"Mommy!" I ran to find her. "Uncle won't let me use the bathroom, and I gotta pee! He's not using the bathroom! He's giving himself a needle!"

My mother asked, "How do you know he's not using the bathroom?"

Uh oh. "Um, um, I saw him through the hole." I'd get in trouble for peeking into the bathroom, but I had to pee!

Finally she got him out of the bathroom for me.

My uncle and his wife had really big, swollen hands and I didn't know why. Was it because they were giving themselves needles that they should be getting from a doctor?

I first met Sonya in kindergarten, and we were still friends in first grade. She often came over to my house to play. Sonya seemed to know more about adult stuff than the other kids in our class, and became a fresh-mouthed little girl who often talked back to the teacher and got into trouble.

There was a coatroom in our classroom, a long closet that children had to walk through to get to the exit. After recess when we came in, we always hung up our coats in the closet and then went into the classroom.

Once when I hung up my coat, Sonya and I were the last ones in the coatroom. Instead of walking to our seats, Sonya wanted to give me a hug, and I let her. But then the hug turned into something more.

Sonya started grinding, rubbing up and down, on my leg. What was she doing? What was this? Was she being a little extra friendly?

In a way, it reminded me of what Cousin Andrew did in the basement, and it felt uncomfortable. When the teacher called for us, Sonya let me go, and we walked back to our seats. She carried on as if nothing was wrong.

What would cause Sonya to behave like that? Who taught her to do it?

I never told anyone.

It happened several times.

When Sonya came to my house to play, my cousin Andrew started being very friendly with Sonya. I didn't know if he touched her in a bad way, but most likely he did.

Why did so many people seem so odd?

My inquisitiveness didn't start, or stop, with peeking at my uncle through the bathroom door. Nor was that the most confusing act I saw.

3 HALLELUJAH

When I was eight years-old my life changed.

It was June 1976 and it was hot. My mother drove me and six of my cousins, whose mother had passed away, to stay with our Aunt Nina (NYNA) in Akron, Ohio, for the summer. Aunt Nina was giving my mother a break from my cousins.

I wanted to go with them because my brothers often got to see their fathers, but I didn't. I didn't know who my father was. I always thought my birth had been an accident. I wasn't supposed to have been born. I was a mistake. Knowing that, *always* knowing that, I wanted to spend one whole summer feeling like I belonged somewhere.

The drive from New Jersey to Akron in my mother's yellow jeep took six hours. We had fun singing songs, talking, and cracking jokes on one another.

Shortly after she dropped us off, my mother drove the six hours back home. She had two jobs. She had to work.

On Sunday morning, Aunt Nina took us to church.

There I watched people do things that I had never seen before. They cried out to the ceiling of the church. They ran around the church like they were crazy. They even spoke another language which was not what I was being taught in school—maybe it was in Spanish, or French, or something.

These people were talking to the ceiling with their eyes closed and they were crying and I just did not understand what was going on.

But I wanted to understand what was going on. Why were people running around the church? Why would someone scream, "Hallelujah! Thank you, Jesus!"?

No matter where I went, I often crossed paths with people whose brains didn't seem to work right. Yet, somehow, these people's actions made more sense to me than the actions of anyone who'd ever hurt me.

We went to that curious place each Sunday.

Once while we were sitting in church, Aunt Nina asked me, "Do you know who Jesus Christ is?"

I looked at her. "Um, no."

She asked, "Do you want to go to heaven?"

Heaven? "What is heaven?"

She said, "Heaven is a beautiful place where the streets are paved with gold and everyone is very nice to you. It's a place where bad things cannot happen to you, a place filled with love, where you can have anything you ever wanted. Heaven is where God lives. It is the best place to be, and you can live forever and ever and never die."

A place filled with love, where you can have anything you ever wanted. Suddenly, hot tears swam in my eyes and caused things to blur. I wanted a daddy. I wanted a daddy who loved me and would come see me and would let me be part of his life. I wanted it terribly, so much that my throat ached.

She asked, "Do you want to go to heaven?"

"Yes!"

"Do you know what has to be done in order to go to heaven?"

"No, what?"

"Pinky, all you have to do is say you're sorry for all the bad things you've done, and you have to accept God and Jesus Christ as your personal savior, and you have to be a good girl. Then you can go to heaven when you die."

I could do most of that! But she'd said a couple of words I hadn't heard before. "Personal Savior?"

"That means you are saved by God and Jesus Christ, and that means when you die you will go to heaven."

I was so excited, because the things she'd told me I had to do seemed really easy, and I wanted to go to heaven.

Aunt Nina asked, "Do you want to be saved?"

My heart felt so full, it felt like it was spilling over, like too much milk in a cup. "Yes, Aunt Nina! I want to be saved! Yes, I believe in God! Yes, I believe in baby Jesus!" Things the man in front of church had been saying began to make a little sense. "Yes, I believe Jesus died for all the bad things I did! Yes! I believe he came back to life! And yes, I believe he went back up to heaven with God and he is watching over me every day."

I accepted Jesus Christ as my Lord and Savior. I cried, telling God that I was sorry for all of the bad things I had done.

Aunt Nina said, "Pinky, you are saved!"

I felt ecstatic. I kept crying, but now they were tears of happiness.

After a couple of weeks, I too was lifting my hands up to the ceiling, praising God and Jesus, and running around the church when the pastor said, "If you love Jesus, run for Jesus!"

I loved my aunt Nina with a special love, because she opened up my heart and mind to someone who could help me so I wouldn't have to be so alone. Thank you, Aunt Nina!

One Sunday Aunt Nina said, "You can learn how to talk like these other people do. It's called speaking in tongues."

I did not understand it, but I knew that I did not want to go to hell because she'd told me that hell was a bad place. I did not want to burn when I died. I did not want to be with all the bad people. I wanted to go to heaven to be with baby Jesus.

"To speak in tongues and talk to God in a special language, all you have to do is to keep saying 'thank you, Jesus' over and over again, and say it fast, and then you'll start speaking in tongues."

So I began to say, "Thank you, Jesus. Thank you Jesus, thankyouJesus!" I believe I started to speak in tongues, but I'm not sure.

Toward the end of summer, I noticed a poster on the wall at church. The words on the poster read, *God doesn't make junk.*

I stopped and stared at those words. Strangely, I felt like the words had been put there especially for me.

God doesn't make junk. I thought about that. God doesn't make mistakes.

God. Doesn't. Make. Mistakes.

I had to keep telling myself that to really start to believe it.

That meant my birth wasn't an accident.

I wasn't a mistake.

God had some purpose for me being born. He had a purpose for me.

I needed to find out what it was.

After the summer ended and I returned home, I gathered my best friends Sonya and Lila together in the basement of my house where we used to play. There I told them about my experience of meeting God, talking to God, and learning about baby Jesus. I told them so they could be saved too. I told them to tell Jesus and God that they were sorry for all the bad things they had done, and that if they believed in God and his Son and that he died for their sins and he rose again, that they were saved.

Then I tried to teach them how to speak in tongues. "Thank you, Jesus. Thank you Jesus, thankyouJesus!"

Amazingly, Sonya started to speak in tongues like the people at church.

We were all overwhelmed and crying and talking to and praising God in our own way. We looked at each other and felt truly special.

I began to understand that God had made each of us special. That he loved each one of us. And I loved him, too.

4 SHADES OF PINK

In third grade, I along with a bully named Anthony, discovered that Pinky can handle herself in a fight.

After completing a writing assignment early, I took my paper up to the teacher's desk and set it in the "finished" box. As I walked down the aisle between the students' desks to return to my seat, Anthony, a thin boy with glasses and a perpetual smirk, reached out and fondled my behind.

I spun and punched him square in the face.

He jumped out of his seat and hit me back. I punched him and punched him and kicked him. I knocked his glasses off his face. They flew across the room.

I kicked his butt for touching mine.

Our crabby teacher, Miss Kaplan, hurried over to separate us. "Stop it! Stop it right now!" Finally she pried us apart. "What happened?"

I told her, "He touched my butt!"

Anthony quickly lied. "No, I didn't."

I said, "Yes, he did!"

"No I didn't."

"Yes he *did*!"

Miss Kaplan yelled at him, "Go to the principal's office!"

He had to go to the nurse to get checked out. Then he got suspended.

During fourth grade, one of my best friends, Veronica, and I got into a minor disagreement.

My so-called friend, Sonya, said, "Let's put their mothers on their shoulders and see who knocks it off." Then they placed a piece of paper on each of our shoulders, and that was supposed to represent our mothers.

We did not want to fight each other, but our "friends" pushed us against each other. Veronica and I had had a disagreement about something small, but we allowed the other girls to get involved.

Once the papers were on each other's shoulders, we halfheartedly taunted each other.

"You knock my mother off the block."

"No, you knock my mother off the block."

We kept saying it, though we knew in our hearts that we did not want to fight each other.

Somebody pushed us together, and the fight began.

I did get the best of her. At one point in the fight, I had her down on the ground, was on top of her, and was about to punch her really hard in the face. God stopped my hand and spoke to me: *No! Don't do it!* I literally heard his voice, out loud, beside me.

I stopped. No one was there but the girls. I stood up and walked home, grateful to God.

I felt really awful about hurting Veronica. The day Anthony fondled my backside, I'd defended myself—I showed him and everyone else that *that* would not be tolerated. But it wasn't in my nature to fight for no reason, and I had allowed other girls to persuade me to do something I didn't want to do.

My friendship with Veronica was never the same again.

I began to realize that Sonya was a big bully and was always trying to get people to fight.

I wondered if she was still listening to God. I don't think so.

When I was nine, I caused a fight at home.

My mother had left a dime on her nightstand. She was adamant about telling us that stealing was wrong, no matter what the item was. If something did not belong to you, you didn't touch it.

I went into my mother's room to get something for her, and that shiny, gleaming dime started calling my name. I knew that I could go to the store and get some candy with that dime, and so I took it and hid it in my room.

A couple of hours later, my mother asked who had taken her dime. No one answered.

"Pinky," she said. "Did you take my dime?"

I was so scared that I lied. "No!"

Unfortunately, I had been the only one in her room, so she knew the truth.

"Pinky! Go get the orange stick!"

We usually kept the orange stick in the living room near the couch, I began to cry because that orange stick hurt.

Once I brought it, my mother grabbed the stick and used it to blister my backside. She hit me again and again. For some reason she would not stop beating me.

My oldest cousin, Leah, grew angry and yelled at my mother. "Stop hitting her! Stop hitting her!!! Over a dime?! She doesn't deserve to get beat like that over a dime!"

A huge argument erupted between the two because my cousin didn't think the beating I received was equal to the crime of taking a dime off of a nightstand.

I felt awful that my cousin and my mother got into a dispute because of what I'd done. I had been wrong. I had stolen the dime.

I silently promised that I would never steal another dime from mother or anyone else.

And yet . . . What had really caused my mother to beat me?

Five years had passed since the first night my cousin Andrew had carried me down to the basement. He had continued to live with us off and on while home from the detention centers. And he had continued to touch me inappropriately and hurt me at night.

He was always getting into a lot of trouble, but I wasn't sure why.

One day at school, a female guest speaker, talked to us students about what she called "good touches" and "bad touches." At last I more clearly understood that the type of touches I had been receiving from my cousin Andrew and from other people were bad touches.

How would I handle this newfound information?

The lady said, "You have to tell someone. Tell the person who's touching you in a bad way, 'Stop!' Tell them, 'No!' Then you have to tell someone else who can stop them from touching you again."

Andrew was still my favorite cousin, and we still spent time together upstairs in his room in the attic. As always, we watched my favorite TV shows and played games there. I had recently turned ten years old.

On a particular day, while we were in the attic watching television, I had been sitting on his lap and had fallen asleep. I awoke with him zipping down my red pants and putting his hand inside my panties.

I remembered what the lady speaker at school had said.

I told Andrew, "No! Stop!" Then I ran downstairs crying. Immediately I called my oldest cousin, Leah, into the bathroom and told her what had happened.

Leah was upset, and very angry. She said, "I am going to handle it! Don't worry about it! It will never happen again!"

She walked out of the bathroom and stormed up into the attic.

I'm not sure what Leah did or said, or who she told, but Cousin Andrew never touched me again.

Thank you, Leah!

Thank you, lady speaker!

Thank you, God!

Andrew's hurting me had not been my fault. I had done nothing wrong.

I told someone, and Cousin Andrew didn't hurt me again.

Actually, I had done something right.

My mother's standing rule was that we don't go outside while she was at work.

For some strange reason, one particular day, my cousins and brothers decided not to obey that rule.

A famous boxer named Muhammad Ali had come to downtown Paterson, New Jersey. He was promoting his upcoming fight.

My cousins and brothers wanted to go see him.

I said, "No! I don't want to go because mommy said to stay in the house."

But because I was younger and smaller than they were, they basically dragged me out of the house and started walking me downtown with them to see Mr. Muhammad Ali. I had one younger sibling, my brother Brent, but he didn't mind going.

I was so mad. "I don't want to go! Mommy said we can't go outside!" Then I told them, "I am going to tell on ya'll!"

However, they told me that I would get into trouble because I was with them.

In those days there were no cell phones, there was no star-69, there was no voicemail or call waiting. If you took the phone off the hook, a caller would receive a busy signal, and it would appear as though someone were home and talking on the phone.

My cousins had decided to take the phone off the hook, just in case my mother called home to check on us.

Of course, my mother called while we were gone, and she continued to call.

No one picked up the phone.

Suspicious, she came home from work. To her surprise, none of her six kids were in the house.

My mother is a very smart woman. She drove downtown and found her six children in that large crowd.

That was the quietest ride home I have ever experienced.

She pulled her yellow jeep into the driveway and turned the engine off. In the house, she told us, "Go to your rooms!" Time passed. About enough time to find her orange stick. Then she called us downstairs, one by one, starting with the oldest.

I was the fifth child out of six. I listened to stick cracks and howling and felt empathy burns on my backside for each of my cousins and one brother.

Then my mother yelled, "*Pinky!*"

I started crying before I even got to my mother.

I told her, "Mommy, I told them I did not want to go, because you said not to go outside!" I pleaded my case like a lawyer, but to no avail. I got my butt beat anyway!

I started trying to run, but she grabbed my wrist. With my free hand, I tried to grab the stick. I ran around in circles as she held my arm, trying to beat me. We went around and around as I tried to stop her from hitting me with that orange stick.

I grabbed for the stick again, which was the wrong thing to do because she hit my hand with the stick, and my thumb began to bleed. (As a matter of fact, I still have a little scar on my thumb.)

Now I realize that my mother must have held back her laughter while watching me run in circles trying not to get hit, because as I think about it, it was hilarious.

It just wasn't hilarious at the time. I don't think Mr. Ali would have wanted to get in the ring with my mother.

5 ORPHAN'S WALLS

(Brent Keys - Brother & Evonne Seldon - Mother)

While growing up, my cousins and brothers knew who their fathers were. Though most of their fathers were abusive, and all but one of their fathers eventually died, they had some type of relationship with them. They had some identity. They belonged to someone.

All my life I wondered who my father was. I could never get a straight answer from my mother.

Once my mother demanded one of my siblings' fathers to take me with them for the day. He refused, because I wasn't his. Although there were times when he did take me with them.

But my mother meant well and though she worked two jobs to support us, she was also an active and fun mom when time allowed. She played kickball games with us and other neighborhood kids on the concrete school playground across the road. She was a lifeguard and taught many kids how to swim at Costello Pool, named after Lou Costello, the famous television show comedian who was also from Paterson.

Perhaps best of all, my mother loved to fish. She often went with my cousins or her friends, and they would bring back buckets full of fish. I wanted to learn how to fish.

On a summer morning when I was ten, my mother packed up her fishing box with hooks, line, weights, pliers, worms she'd bought, and all kinds of other fishing gear. She also collected her white bucket and her two fishing poles. Then she looked at us kids who were just hanging out.

"Anyone want to go with?" she asked.

I jumped up. "Yes!"

None of my siblings said anything. They were content to stay at home.

My mother told me, "Hurry up and get yourself ready to go."

A few minutes later, my mother and I climbed into her yellow jeep and headed down the road.

Finally, I had special time that I could spend with my mother and have her all to myself. I felt excited to go fishing with her.

During the forty-minute ride, we listened to our favorite songs on her 8-track music tapes of Marvin Gaye's *Let's Get It On*, The Spinners' *I'll Be Around* and *Could It Be I'm Falling in Love*, the Chi-Lites' *Oh Girl*, and Harold Melvin & the Blue Notes' *If You Don't Know Me by Now*. We sang loud and laughed while she drove.

My mother taught me how to fish with one of her two poles. I bubbled with enthusiasm over every moment of the day, including casting. After about the fifth time she pried my hook out of a tree in the thicket, I bubbled with enthusiasm as she taught me how to fish with a line tied around the middle of an inert soda can.

I held the ends of the empty Coca-Cola can in my hands while she tied an orange and yellow bobber, a silver weight, and a hook onto my soda can's fishing line.

She taught me how to put the nasty, squirmy little worm on the hook too. At first I felt sorry for sticking the hook through the worm, but then I started to enjoy putting the worm on the hook because I was excited about catching some fish.

Then my mother provided new casting instructions. "Slowly swing the line with its hook and bobber around in circles, then twirl it a little faster, and then release it toward the water."

It worked! My bobber sat on top the river, and the hook and worm sank beneath it.

"Now sit patiently and watch to see if your bobber goes down or if your fishing line jerks."

I did what she told me to do. She took up her pole, cast out her line, and sat beside me.

We sat quietly together.

Sounds of birds, the river, and flying insects held my attention for a time. Then my thoughts, as was typical for me, grew curious.

"Ma, how did you learn how to fish? Did your mother teach you?"

Though she didn't move, she suddenly seemed stiffer.

"No. My mother didn't teach me how to fish."

Her face had the same look it got whenever I asked her who my father was.

She kept her attention on the river. "I guess you're old enough to learn about how I grew up."

For once I held back the questions, and listened.

"Pinky, I taught myself how to fish when I lived at an orphanage.

"You lived at an orphanage?" The thought stunned me.

She nodded. "My own mother—your Grandmother Doreen— was young when she had her first child. She was pregnant at fourteen years old, and married and a mama at fifteen. By the time she was twenty, she had five children.

"My father—that's your Grandfather Ernest—was a boxer, a little like Rocky Balboa or Apollo Creed. But he had to tour the region to box, so he lived away more than he lived at home. He was also a very good pool shark. That's someone who plays pool for money."

Her fishing line had drifted. She reeled it in then recast it a little further upstream.

She continued. "Your grandfather was an African American man. Your grandmother is multiracial, including African American, White, and Indian. I'm not sure what happened in their marriage, but one day while my father was away, my mother asked a friend to babysit us. Then my mother left. Three days later our babysitter called the police, and the five of us children were taken into Child Protective Services. That means they took us away from home.

"When my mother came to get us, she was told that my two older sisters, Henrietta and Geraldine, had ringworm, and that my baby sister, Tinesha, had pneumonia. They said my younger brother, Ernell, and I appeared to be healthy. So my mother took her three sick children home with her. She left Ernell and me there at the Child Protective Services shelter for children."

Just then it seemed like the anger in her eyes could have burned water.

"When my father discovered my mother had taken only three of us five children home with her, he reacted badly, as you might expect—my mother told me a little about it a few years ago, though she wouldn't say much. It's rare that she'll discuss her past at all. Anyway, she finally came back to pick up Ernell and me. But my father had ordered some kind of restriction to stop her from getting us. Yet, because he was often on the road boxing, he didn't come get us out of the shelter to take care of us either!

"I don't know everything that happened," she said. "I was way too young to understand it all, and my mother won't talk much about it, like I said. But we stayed in the Child Protective Services shelter until we were about four and five years old. Then we were driven to a place called Lakeside School and Orphanage, which is in Spring Valley, New York. We had a house mother and father who were white and in charge of the facility."

One of the questions in my thoughts slipped out. "What was the orphanage like?"

Her mouth went flat. "About five hundred kids lived there, nearly all of them white. I clearly remember my first day there. I had just walked into the home when the house father grabbed my arm and took me into the bathroom. He pushed and held my head down over the sink with one hand and with the other started raking through my hair with a tiny tooth comb that was not meant for black hair. My hair was too thick, but he yanked the comb through it anyway.

"I started struggling hard—I was scared and screaming— because I saw bugs—lice—drop out of my hair and he kept tearing at my scalp with that comb." A bird flew down to the river, took a drink, and then left again. "Seeing those lice really traumatized me. I started having horrific nightmares."

"About lice?"

"Actually, about snakes. I dreamed they were everywhere, crawling all over me while I slept." She shuddered. "I don't know why. I began to see snakes when I was awake too. Snakes in the corners of my room, snakes moving on my bed, snakes coiled on and in my pillow. . . . I saw them everywhere. I believed I was in a bed full of snakes every night.

"I'd wake up in the middle of the night screaming at the top of my lungs and crying, which woke and scared the other children. I shrieked so loud I woke kids sleeping in the other buildings."

"How long did you see snakes?"

"For months. The kids took to teasing me and calling me a nigger. I told the counselors and staff members what was happening, but they didn't do enough to stop the kids from calling me names and picking on me. They wouldn't stop, so that is how I learned to defend myself." My mother nodded. "Yes, I took matters into my own hands—literally. The orphanage is where I learned how to fight, and it's also where I learned how to cuss. The white kids taught me how to cuss, and I did that very well."

"You still do," I assured her.

Her mouth started to grin, but she kept it from spreading and raised an eyebrow at me. "It became a defense mechanism. I would beat kids up for calling me a nigger, even though I didn't know what the word meant at that time. I just knew it wasn't a good word, and I didn't like it.

"One time, the director of Lakeside told me I should come tell him the next time someone called me a nigger. I said, 'I'll come tell you after I kick their ass!' I had to fight to defend myself. I was eight years old."

"How many fights did you have? Who did you fight? What happened?"

My mother shared a story about when she shared a bedroom with 11 other girls in the orphanage, and they had to gain points in order to move to a different room with fewer girls.

"A little white girl continued to call me a nigger when it was bedtime. I said to her if you call me a nigger one more time; I am going to kick you in your eye! The little white girl said 'nigger!' I got out of my bed and walked over to the girls' bed; I picked up my foot, and I kicked her in the eye!

The little girl screamed and cried, and the house father came running into the bedroom and asked what happened? While screaming, crying, and pointing at me, she told the House father, 'she kicked me in my eye! She kicked me in my eye!'

I tried to run away and hide, but the house father began to chase me. I ran as fast I could around the bedroom, and he cornered me by the closet door and he grabbed me by my arm.

As I was fighting him and trying to get away from him, he grabbed me. I fell to the floor, kicking and screaming; he grabbed my legs as she was kicking him yelling, 'Get off me! Get off me! Let me go! Let me go!'

He grabbed my legs and feet and once he got a firm grip; he dragged me. As he was dragging me, I was trying to grab and hold onto the closet door handle, the curtains; the bed spread/covers, the bed posts anything that would stop him from dragging me and taking me out of the room. I continued to scream 'Let me go! Let me go! She called me a nigger! She called me a nigger!'"

As he was dragging me across the floor, I was holding onto the frame of the door, and he continued to pull and drag me. My head hit the other frame of another door very hard. Bam! I was screaming and crying even more because it hurt. I had a huge knot /bump on my forehead. I continued to scream 'Let me go!'

He picked me up and carried me to the bathroom; I was still fighting and trying to get away from him. 'Let me go! Let me go!' He turned the cold water on in the shower and threw me in a cold shower where I continued to scream and cry. 'It is cold in here! AHH! It is cold in here!!!! AHH! It is cold!!!!' Shivering, screaming and crying. 'I am telling my father on you! I am telling my father on you! Let me out of here!!! Let me out of here!!! Let me out of here!!!"

The house father finally let me out of the cold shower. I continued to cry and scream. I was not taken to the infirmary to get my head checked. He then he tried to calm me down. The house father put some ice on my head to try and bring down the swelling.

In the midst of all of this I was still screaming and crying and I, yelled at the house father 'my father is going to come here and kick your ass! She called me a nigger! My father is going to come here and kick your ass!' The swelling of the bump on my head went down. So I went back to bed. I could have had a concussion. They did not care! They were supposed to take care of me and take me to the infirmary to see a doctor, but they did not."

I became sad for my mommy as she told that story. My mother shared another story.

(Ernell - Age 6, Mother – Age 7, and her best friend Irene – Age 7)

"When I was about eight years old, this big white boy named George, who was about 15 years old, constantly called me nigger. I would cuss at him and constantly called him a motherfucker. He would get angry. This went on for several days.

One day he got very angry, and he called me a nigger and I called him a motherfucker. He walked over to me; made a fist and swung his fist back and forth, and he punched me in the stomach so hard that it knocked the wind out of me. Boom! Boom!

I fell back and began to cry and scream. I was gasping for air because I had trouble breathing. Although he was bigger, older and stronger than me, I was still gasping for air, and I was still able to call him a MO (breath) TH (breath) ER (breath) FU (breath) CK (breath) ER! In between each breath I was trying to take. He was still angry with me as I stood there crying.

Another white boy named Richard saw me crying and asked 'What's the matter? What happened?' I told him, and Richard ran over to George and commenced to kicking his ass! Richard kicked his ass! For me! Richard said to me that 'if he calls you that name again I will kick his ass over and again, every time! So make sure you tell me if he bothers you again,' as I looked at George beat up and bloodied on the floor, I licked my tongue at him. George never called me a nigger or bothered me again. I thanked Richard.

"Mommy, you was a fighter and did not back down when you were eight years old. Wow! Did grandpa come and kick their butts?"

"No."

"Did your mother or father ever visit you?" Maybe she had visits from her parents like my brothers and cousins had from their fathers.

"Lakeside had friends and family visitation days on Saturdays and Sundays," she answered. "The other kids' parents and family members came and visited them, and my father and mother came for a couple of visits, but not often. I began to realize that my parents weren't coming to see my brother and I as regularly as they should have, like the other children's parents. That hurt bad.

When visitation hours began and all of the friends and family members walked in to visit with the other kids, I'd run outside and run deep into the woods to hide by my favorite tree. I'd sit there and cry my eyes out. I'd cry and talk to God and ask him to help me. I'd ask, 'Where are my mommy and daddy? Why don't they come visit me and my brother? Why am I here?' Many times when I was there crying and praying, I felt peace settle over me, sort of like a big, soft blanket. God helped me to stop crying. I walked back up to the orphanage after visitation was over.

"After a while, instead of always going to my favorite tree, I'd sometimes go fishing. That's how I learned to fish well. Fishing became something enjoyable I could do."

"How did you hear about God?"

"We went to chapel on a regular basis. I learned about God there, but I felt closest to him when I was hurting and crying in the woods.

"I had no idea what a mother and father should be like until I was eight or nine years old. I still don't know why my parents didn't get me out of that place. It was terrible. No child should have to grow up like that.

The orphanage sounded like an awful place, where there was no love and a lot of sadness. It sounded like the place called hell that Aunt Nina talked about.

Maybe that was why my mother let our cousins live with us after their mother died, I reasoned, and why she always let so many other people live with us. Crowded was better than orphaned.

My mother said, "If any of the house parents or counselors at Lakeside had paid some attention to the good in me, they would have realized I had talents. I wished they had encouraged me to play more tennis, because I was a good tennis player and would win almost every tennis match against the children and the adults. Now, Pinky, you know I don't condone boasting, but I was good at it, and that's just a fact."

I nodded. She was good at kickball and swimming and other sports, too.

"I was a good swimmer even then, and I helped teach some of the other kids how to swim. But neither the house parents nor the counselors nor my parents ever encouraged my talents. Yet they were quick enough to tell us kids when we did something wrong. It was not an easy life."

The fishing line around my soda can began to jerk. In the river, my yellow and orange bobber dipped, then almost disappeared under the water. I jumped up in excitement and started jumping around and screaming, "Mommy, I got something! I got something!"

"Roll your can! Roll your can to reel in your line!"

I almost dropped the can into the water, but my mother managed to catch it and swiftly began to roll the can and reel in the fish. When we could see the fish splashing in the water, my mother let me reel it the rest of the way in.

I was so excited and kept jumping around. "I caught a fish! I caught a fish!" The fish was somersaulting around in the air, but my hook was stuck in its mouth so it couldn't get away.

My mother steered me toward the tackle box and used her pliers to get the hook out of the fish's mouth. Then she released it in her bucket of water.

I couldn't believe it. I'd caught a fish!

"Nice catch, Pinky, but we need enough so that everyone at home can have dinner. Let's fish some more."

We sat down again and cast out our lines with new worms on our hooks. She caught a fish of her own only a few minutes later, then put it in the bucket and got another worm.

Her mother, my grandmother, hadn't taught her how to fish. I thought about my mother at the orphanage. "How long did you live at that place?"

(Evonne Seldon – Mother – Age 13)

"Until I was twelve. Around then, my father went to the Child Protective Services court and had full custody of Ernell and me given to his cousin, Eva. We called her Aunt Eva. That woman abused the two of us—physically, mentally, emotionally, and spiritually—in ways that were unthinkable.

"Once, I cut my brother's hair for him. I made a mistake and cut too much hair, and he ended up with a bald spot in his hair. I was so scared. Aunt Eva found out. She beat me with something called a cat o' nine tails, a kind of whip. The cat was made up of nine knotted cords, thick like extension cords, with bits of sharp metals at the ends of the cords that are designed to tear the skin and cause severe pain. She beat me so hard with the cat o' nine tails that some of the wire from the cord was embedded in my arm."

My mother's face had turned sort of a gray, chalky color.

She said, "As I was being beaten, I would bleed from the cuts, and Aunt Eva would yell at me to clean the blood off the floor—and she'd expect me to do it while she continued to beat me." She slowly shook her head. "I could never understand why my father would give us to this crazy woman. I wondered where my mother was.

"And you know what was even worse? Aunt Eva had a sister named Ida who would give us another beating *because* we got one from Aunt Eva. Fortunately, Aunt Ida's beatings were not as bad as Aunt Eva's. I often wondered, '*Why* do the people who live in the downstairs apartment not call the police?!' My screams were so loud! I could not believe that no one would do anything about it. And we got beaten for just about anything that Aunt Eva considered wrong. It was cruel! And no one came to save my brother and me."

My head felt strange, and I didn't really notice my bobber. Why had those people done that to my mother?

"While Ernell and I lived there, an old woman, who looked very much like a white woman because her skin was very light, came to visit Aunt Eva's apartment with a black baby. I remember thinking, 'Who is this old white woman with this black baby?' But Aunt Eva never introduced us to the woman.

"A couple of years later, Ernell and I went to a funeral with Aunt Eva. As we walked into the funeral home and sat down, I heard people saying, 'She looks just like her mother!' At first I didn't know who they were talking about. Then I noticed that they were talking about me, that I was the one who looked like my mother. Thinking my mother might be there, I looked around to see if I could find someone in the audience who resembled me, but I couldn't.

"Later I found out that the funeral I attended was for my great-grandmother—the old "white" woman who had come to the apartment carrying the black baby."

"Who was the baby?"

"She was my little sister."

My mother reeled in another fish then baited and cast out her hook again. She seemed sad.

"I found out later that my grandmother had lived only three blocks from us, but no one had ever told me. My grandmother never hugged Ernell or me, or acknowledged that we were her grandchildren.

"And all those people at the funeral? Some of them were my family—my siblings and my mother. Nobody told me that the day of the funeral either. Eventually I learned that I had eight additional brothers and sisters who I didn't get to grow up with. My mother had thirteen children now, but Ernell and I didn't live with them. And though my family members visited my grandmother regularly, they never came to see Ernell and me just three blocks away.

"Pinky, I understand you're wanting to know your father. I wanted to get to know my mother and meet my eight new brothers and sisters when I was just a little older than you."

I felt hopeful. Maybe my mother would finally tell me who my father was.

"I guess I'll tell you the rest of it, because I don't like to talk about it or even think about it. In that respect, I might not be all that different from my mother."

"Okay."

"One day my oldest sister, Henrietta, came to visit Ernell and me at Aunt Eva's house. She asked if he and I could go to the movies with her. I didn't know it then, but Henrietta had ran away from home. I got a beating from Aunt Eva because she thought I knew Henrietta was a runaway and wasn't going to tell her.

"Henrietta left, but her running away had given us an idea. After years of being abused by Aunt Eva, Ernell and I ran away from home. We were about fifteen and sixteen. He and I found a fully furnished model mobile home that we stayed in. We hid under a bed when realtors brought in potential buyers, and used the bathrooms and slept in the beds when they left.

"We'd go to local stores and steal food, clothes, and toiletries—things we needed. Two weeks after we ran away, the cops found us hiding underneath one of the beds of the model mobile home."

Wow, that must have been scary! "What did the police do?"

"They took us back to Aunt Eva's house. Almost immediately Aunt Eva sent my brother to live with some of our family in Pennsylvania, and sent me back to Child Protective Services. CPS transferred me to Hutchins State Home for Girls. And *they* relocated me to the Valley Stream Home for Girls in Long Island, New York.

"When I was seventeen, I was placed in a foster home. The foster mother had a daughter around my age. That woman would not buy me any clothes with the money that she received from the state to take care of me. I had to wear winter clothes all through the summer!

"When the foster mother cooked dinner, the food that anyone left on their plates after eating she'd scrape back into the pot and serve it for dinner the next day. That was nasty! I could not handle that! I badly wanted to get out of there. Not long after I arrived, the foster mother's daughter became pregnant and decided she was no longer going to school, I said, 'If she ain't going to school, I ain't neither!' Around then I met my soon-to-be husband and left. And I began to communicate with my real mother."

"Was he my father?"

"No, that was Robert, your older brothers' father. Robert and I dated, I became pregnant, and then had your brother Lonnie. Times were hard. I wrote and asked my mother—she'd moved from New York to Paterson, New Jersey—if my boyfriend and my month-old baby boy could come and live with her until we got on our feet. She said yes. So we came here."

We looked at our bobbers in the river. I was afraid to ask her anything else, because she'd already told me a lot, and she often grew impatient with my questions. But she had to be close to the part where she met my father. "Then you got married to Robert, right?"

"Well, we lived with my mother a couple of months, then moved around Paterson for a time. I married Robert when I was in my early twenties.

"But you didn't stay married to him."

"Like a lot of people, he was nice at first. Then he started…Well, not coming home all the time. After that, I didn't stay married to him long. Eventually I found more boyfriends and ended up having more children.

"Did you know, I went to college and took some classes at Bank Street College in New York and at Jersey City College in Jersey City? I got a job as corrections officer at one of the youth detention centers in Paterson. Did you know, I once intercepted a possible stabbing from one of the youths?"

I shook my head. I'd never heard that before. "You took the knife away from him?"

"Well, I convinced him to turn over a plastic knife that he was trying to smuggle from the cafeteria. He'd had problems with some of the other inmates and wanted to defend himself. I told him that using that knife would make things worse for him. He handed me the knife, and so no one was harmed.

"You see? It's important to never give up on anyone. Not even yourself, or you'll never get out of any bad situation you might be in."

I'd respected my mother before. Now I respected her even more.

But she still hadn't told me who my father was.

"Mommy—"

"Pinky, be patient! I'm getting to the part about your dad. But you needed to understand about your sisters' and brother's dads first, right?" She sighed at my impatience and reeled in another fish.

I was afraid to say anything, even to agree with her, for fear she'd be too frustrated with me and not tell me. So I just sat holding my soda can, hoping I'd catch a big fish to please her so she would be willing to tell me.

"I met your father in a bar. Olin. His name is Olin."

Olin? My real name was Olandha—like a girl version of Olin! I had been named after my father, like two of my brothers had been named after other fathers!

"Olin and I talked and got to know each other. He and I went on two or three dates, and on the last date we decided to . . . Sleep together. You know what I mean?"

Not exactly, but I said, "I think so."

"One time and one time only! But, I became pregnant with you.

"I told your father that I'd become pregnant. He didn't believe me because we only once— well, he didn't believe me. And then he told me that he was married."

I sat quietly and tried to understand what it all meant. She was shaking her head, though I wasn't sure she realized she was doing it.

She said, "I was devastated. If I'd known earlier that he was married, I would have never dated him!

"Anyway, we had an argument. Somewhere in the middle of it, I asked him, 'Are you going to take care of your responsibilities?'"

"What does that mean?"

"Be a dad to you and things. He said yes, he would. But he never has.

"When you were born, you were a light-skinned baby. I bundled you up and took you over to the bowling alley where your father and his brothers bowled every Saturday. They were part of a bowling league. Anyway, I walked over to him, took the blanket off of your face, and showed you to your father. He didn't believe you could be his baby because your skin was so light.

"I swore at him walked away. Then I saw his brothers, Eddie and Moose, so I went over to them and showed you to them. They said, 'Yes, she looks just like him and his youngest daughter.'"

It felt like something sharp struck my heart just then. I even looked like my father!

My mother glanced at me with concern. "Do you want me to stop telling you?"

"No," I said.

"After that, I ran into Eddie and Moose sometimes. They told me they often harassed Olin about not taking care of his responsibilities, but Olin wouldn't step up to the plate."

She pushed the hair back from her face, then kept her hand on top her head, like she couldn't decide whether to keep talking or not and her hand was helping her to make up her mind. Her hand returned to her fishing pole.

She said, "Once when you were about five months old, I took you to the doctor for one of your regular well-baby visits. We waited in the sitting room, and I joined a conversation with other mothers there with their children. We were talking about fathers and things, and someone asked me who your father was. I told them your father was Olin. Then one of the mothers who knew him told me that Olin's wife was a nurse right there at that doctor's office! I was stunned. I immediately picked you up and left, and then changed doctors.

"The Paterson medical community is pretty small, even though it has two hospitals. It's likely your father's wife had either held you or at least taken your vitals.

"Maybe now you can see why it's not something I usually talk about."

Birds fluttered, insects hummed, the river gurgled.

I'd wanted my mother to tell me, and she'd told me. I didn't understand many things she'd said, but now I pretty much understood what my siblings meant when they cruelly teased me and said I had a long lost father.

I caught two more fish, and my mother and I sang songs again during the drive back home. After that, I went fishing with her just about every weekend. I loved our special time together.

I had a father, but he didn't want me. Yet I couldn't help asking my mother more and more questions about him.

6 CONFLICT

My mother's face seemed stern as a statue's. "Pinky, get in the car."

Minutes later we arrived at a bowling alley. I followed her inside, and she walked up to a counter, to a short, dark-skinned man sitting on a tall stool. The man wore bowling shoes, jeans, and a checkered shirt.

She said, "Olandha, this Olin, your father. Olin, this is your daughter." Then she walked away from me.

He looked at me, and I looked at him, our eyes wide open in shock.

He stared, and did not say anything to me.

I sat down at the counter next to him. My inquisitiveness broke the silence. "Hi."

"Hi."

"Where have you been?" I asked. "Why haven't you been around to take care of me?"

At first he didn't answer. Then he said, "Well, I don't know if I'm your father."

"Oh. Well, okay." I continued to look at him, and he continued to look at me. What was I supposed to say or do now? How do you talk to someone you don't know?

Neither of us said anything else. We just stared at each other, listening to bowling alley noises like crashes and shatters.

After about five minutes, my mother came back over to us. She looked at both of us, grabbed my hand, and we left the bowling alley.

We got into the car. She slammed her door. "What happened? What did he say?"

"He said he didn't know if he was my father."

"*What?* Then what did you say?"

"I said okay or something."

"That was it?" she yelled. "You didn't say anything more to him?"

"I didn't know what to say!"

"Well, why not?"

Why did she leave me with him? And why was she so mad at me? My insides felt shaky. "Mommy, I don't know!"

She started hollering, cursing, and saying things that I didn't understand.

At home I just cried, feeling very, very, very sad and confused. I was really confused now because I didn't know if my daddy was my daddy. My mother told me that that man was my father. He told me that he didn't know if he was my father. What was I supposed to do now? I really felt lost. And I felt like a burden.

My heart hurt. I didn't understand this. Why was I being punished? What did I do wrong? Why did my mother think I would know what to say and do?

God, help me, please!

During sixth grade I became very active in school. For the most part I was well liked by my teachers and peers. However, a couple of girls seemed jealous that I stayed involved in so many activities.

One of the girls, Melinda, told her older sister, Mallory, and their neighbor, Carly, that I'd said something mean about them that I hadn't. Mallory and Carly, well known for being bullies and beating kids up, were both two years older than me.

After school they approached me and accused me about what Melinda had told them. I told them that I hadn't said it, then I headed home.

As I walked, they followed me with a crowd of people behind them, all of them calling out and talking smack.

I didn't say anything. I just kept walking.

Thank God I lived across the street from school, because when we arrived at my front walkway, they turned around and went back. I had been *so* scared!

Inside our living room, my cousin Olivia, an eighth grader, faced me. She'd seen and heard what had happened. "Pinky, you better not let her punk you in front of all those people. If she bothers you tomorrow, you better fight her back."

I admit—Carly scared me. She came from a family of siblings who liked to fight neighborhood kids, and that was not in my nature. I'd defended myself from a boy who'd fondled my bottom, but I hadn't thought about fighting him.

The next day I did not want to go to school. But I prayed and went.

When I walked in, kids told me that Carly was planning to beat me up.

I told my teacher that Carly and Mallory had followed me home the day before and what the other kids told me Carly planned. My teacher did nothing.

That afternoon, as I left the girls' bathroom, Carly walked up to me with a crowd behind her. She said, "I'm going to kick your ass!" and swung.

A fight erupted in the hallway outside the lunchroom.

Kids were everywhere, watching and instigating and yelling, "Fight! Fight! Fight!"

Carly got the best of me by hitting and punching me. She ripped some beaded braids out of my hair! And she tore out some of my hair!

Gym teachers came running and pulled us apart.

I was crying, I was so mad! I was so mad! I was so mad!

The gym teacher holding me back asked, "Are you okay? Are you okay?"

I nodded. "Yes! I'm okay! You can let me go now."

Wrong!

He let me go. I ran over to Carly and I hit her so hard that I slapped the taste buds out of her mouth! We started fighting again.

This time they had to pull me off of her! I was no longer scared. I was infuriated because I had done nothing wrong to her, nor did I say anything about her!

Chaos filled the hallway with kids going crazy because no one expected little Pinky to do anything like that! They'd thought I was a punk. Surprise!

Once the gym teachers broke us up again, we were both sent home, but Carly got suspended because she started the fight. But I finished it.

Thankfully I was not kicked out of the extracurricular activities I was in because my principal and my teachers knew my character. They knew that I was a good girl and I was honest. Plus, I had talked to my teacher ahead of time and shared what was going on. She just hadn't done anything about it.

When I was twelve and in seventh grade, I became more outgoing and active in sports like my mother had been. As a hardworking student, I earned the trust to be the teacher's and principal's helper, as well as a crossing guard.

Mr. Wiesel, a minister for a local church, worked part time as security guard for the school and as head of the crossing guards. He always smiled, was friendly to all the kids, and regularly gave us hugs.

One Friday after all the kids had been crossed on their way home from school, I turned in my junior patrol equipment to Mr. Wiesel. He wanted to give me a hug goodbye for the weekend.

He hugged me tightly and I hugged him back, but then he wouldn't let me go. As he kept holding me, his hands moved downward. Then he squeezed my bottom.

Wrestling his arms away, I told him, "No! Stop!" and shoved him back from me. I glared at him and left.

Two weeks later, my friend and fellow crossing guard, Carmen, came to me shaking and in tears. She told me that Mr. Wiesel had hugged her close and had touched her bottom.

I left her and went to find Mr. Wiesel, whose desk sat directly in front of the principal's office door. Mr. Wiesel would be there around this time.

Predators, it seemed, preferred to target the weak. The defenseless. The quiet. Those who would be too afraid to tell. After all, what predator would risk ambushing prey that was certain to strike back or too loudly reveal their actions?

I was done being quiet.

Mr. Wiesel sat at his desk. The secretary's door stood open. The principal's door stood open.

I stopped in front of Mr. Wiesel's desk. "If you ever touch me or my friend Carmen on our bottoms again, I will tell the principal! Is that what you do to the girls at your church?"

Mr. Wiesel looked like he was about to have a heart attack.

I walked away.

As far as I know, he never touched Carmen again. I know he never touched me again!

People who did bad things like this, I now knew, could be ministers, neighbors, friends, family members, and people at school—both adults and other kids. I began to realize that there were many people who weren't safe to be around.

I didn't tell the principal directly. But I should have.

***

Donald, my mother's boyfriend, lived with us for a while. He was the closest thing that I ever had to a father at my home, because he was nice to me, he talked with me about my day at school and my activities, and he did not touch me inappropriately (thank God!).

When I think of Donald today, I still smile, and I smile because he made me smile and laugh.

He had false teeth and would talk to me without his teeth. He'd mimic cartoon characters, he'd mimic me to make me laugh, and he came up with hilarious jokes.

On a Saturday morning after we finished our chores, Donald and I sat out on the front steps to enjoy the warm weather. Across the street kids played baseball on the schools cement playground where my mother sometimes played kickball with us and the neighbor kids.

The warm day was nice, but my thoughts wandered to things that made me sad.

Donald asked, "What's the matter?"

I told him, "I want to know who my father is, and I don't know who he is. I want to get to meet him. I want to get to talk with him!"

"Pinky, do you know that your father is a very good friend of mine?"

I stood up and stared at Donald. "You know my father? But how?"

Donald stared back at me, mimicking my expression to make me smile. "You've already met him, Pinky. At the bowling alley."

"But how could you know he's my father when he told me that he isn't sure? How do you know him?"

"He and I bowl together and hang out at the Elks bar. He and I were friends even back when he met your mother. So? Do you want to know where your father is?"

"Yes!"

"Really? Are you sure?"

"Yes!" My smile got huge.

He'd brought out a newspaper and pencil to work the crossword puzzle. He wrote on a corner of the newspaper, then tore off the corner and gave it to me.

It was a series of numbers. "What's this?"

"Silly. What you think it is?"

"I don't know!"

"That's your father's telephone number."

I gasped in surprise! I was flabbergasted! I was elated! I was happy! I gripped the piece of paper tighter. "Are you for real?"

"Yes!"

I truly couldn't believe that this scrap of paper held my father's telephone number! I stared at it in disbelief. Then I started to believe it. All I had to do was dial just seven numbers and I could speak to my father. "Thank you, Donald!"

My hands held onto to that phone number. I looked at it, and looked at it.

Donald asked, "What are you going to do with it?"

"I am going to call him!"

"Good. Good for you! Call him! You deserve to know who your father is!"

Instead of calling, I sat back down, staring at the telephone number.

Was Olin really my father? When I was ten years old, he told me that he didn't know if he was. But my mother said he was. Was Donald mistaken, or was he right?

A little while later, I put the piece of paper in a cubbyhole shelf by my bed.

Two days after, when no one else was around, I walked into the kitchen, worked up some courage, and dialed the telephone number. Nervous, I began to pace while I listened into to the phone.

It rang once. No one answered it.

It rang again. Then someone picked up the phone.

A woman's voice said, "Hello?"

Maybe this was my father's wife, the nurse who'd probably held me when I was a baby.

"Can I speak to Olin, please?"

"Hold on."

I heard voices through the phone, then, "Hello?"

"Hi. I'm Olandha, Evonne's daughter."

"Uh, how are you doing in school?" He sounded like he was trying to play it off as if I were someone else, maybe his and his wife's daughter.

"I'm fine."

"Okay then. I'll talk to you later." He hung up.

Over the following months, I called that number several times. The same thing happened with each call.

Then a day came when I called again, and the operator told me the number had been changed—to a private number.

She said she couldn't give me the number unless it was an emergency, but that if I gave her my telephone number, she could call the private number and give them my number for them to call me back.

I gave her my number. Olin never called me back.

He didn't want me.

I always tried to be a good person. Why didn't my father want me?

In 1981 I turned thirteen—no longer a child. I wasn't the only one who thought so.

For years an elderly friend of the family had lived with us and paid rent to my mother. His bedroom shared a mutual wall with mine. He took a strong liking to me, and often sent me to the store to buy things for him, then gave me the change left over. Sometimes the change totaled more than five dollars, sometimes more than ten, and sometimes he'd give me twenty-five dollars, just because.

When he needed to, he used a cane to walk. He had very big hands and knobby, arthritic knuckles that stood out when he held the cane.

On afternoons that I didn't have much homework, I kept him company in his room. We talked a lot and watched TV.

For years he had left the door open while we talked. Now he closed the door and asked me to sit on his lap during our chat.

While I sat on his lap and told him about my school day, I noticed that his penis became hard. I tried to stand up, but he held me firmly on him. He moved his big, gnarled hand under my shirt and touched my breasts. I pushed at him, but he turned me from sitting on his lap to lying on him in the chair. He kissed my mouth—I held my lips together—and he rubbed his hard penis against my vaginal area.

There was a tingling sensation, and I felt horribly uncomfortable. Finally I got free.

How could I ever explain this to my mother? She was often stressed and impatient, and she respected this man!

He'd manipulated me with money and attention like a few other bad people had, but I still hadn't realized what he was doing. I'd thought he was being kind. He had been like a grandfather to me.

I didn't tell. But I stopped going to see him.

***

During eighth grade, as a school patrol/crossing guard, I began to get to school on time. More active than ever, I liked learning, loved my teachers, did my work early, and was able to help the teachers when they needed it.

In my home economics class I became one of the better cooks, I was captain of the cheerleading squad, and I was the head member of a dance troupe that danced for assemblies. My older cousin Leah taught us the dance moves, and we did a great job. I was also a member of the choir that sang for graduations. I was physically fit and won several of the physical education class competitions.

I thought that if I always did my best, my father might be so proud of me that he'd finally want me as a daughter.

Then I would tell him, "Daddy, this is what I've done, and this is why you can be proud of me."

For the most part, I continued to be well liked by my peers.

Unfortunately, one group of girls decided that I thought I was better than everybody else. They began to taunt me in an effort to force me to fight them.

I was keen enough to know that I had to follow the rules set by the school, teachers, and the principal. Those rules stated that if a student got into trouble or fought with other students, they could not participate in extracurricular activities or hold leadership positions.

I had more to lose than they did, because I was very involved and they weren't.

Many times those girls (including my best friend Sonya from kindergarten) created rumors and talked about me like a dog. It really hurt my feelings.

One rumor they created brought me to tears. They went around the whole school and told everybody that I stuffed my bra with tissue. Other students began to pick on me. I went home crying and told my mother what happened.

She said, "Take one of the girls into the bathroom with you, lift up your shirt and bra, and show her your breasts so that they'll know you are not stuffing your bra with tissue or socks or anything else."

My heart skipped a beat. My mother was insane.

But I did what she said. The rumors quickly stopped.

Apparently, my mother was a very smart woman.

Near the end of eighth grade, I had my last elementary school fight with a girl named Ann.

Ann hung out with Sonya and the other mean girls. These girls really had it out for me. They did not like the fact that I was outgoing, didn't hang out with the bad kids, and was not a follower. A number of boys liked me— including a couple of their boyfriends—even though I wasn't having sex with them like some of the girls were.

As I walked down the hallway at school, these girls often yelled negative things about me. I would not respond. Eventually they realized I wasn't going to fight them in school because I had more to lose than they did.

Things got worse, to the point that we went to court because of the bullying going on. The judge explicitly told the girls to leave me alone or they would suffer severe consequences.

The bullying slowed down tremendously, but they continued to do subtle things like write trash about me in the girls' bathroom.

One Saturday afternoon I walked to downtown Paterson with my three-year-old nephew. We went into the Ellison Street pizza shop to get a snack.

I heard Ann's voice call, "Look! Here comes the bitch! Look at this bitch!"

Ignoring her, I bought pizza and drinks for my nephew and me. As I walked out the door, I twisted my ass in front of her, and said, "Bye, bitch!"

Unfortunately for her, she stood up and started talking smack.

All of a sudden my soda hit her in the face and we begin to fight inside the pizza store. I blacked out and commenced kicking her butt.

I remember the pizza shop owner screaming, "Get out of my store!" I remember a woman screaming, "Get off my car!"

Somebody broke up the fight, and when I was finished, Ann had bruises and scratches all over her face.

I grabbed my nephew's hand, picked up our pizza, and walked home.

On Monday morning, the fight was the big topic of discussion around the school.

My teacher, Miss Pugatch, pulled me aside and told me she was proud of the fact that I stood up for myself.

After the fight, those girls pretty much left me alone. However, they continued to dislike me. When the time came to sign our yearbooks, a couple of boys looking at the photographs said they thought I was the prettiest girl in our class. Some of those girls didn't like that, so they took erasers and erased my picture out of their yearbooks.

Yes, my feelings were very hurt, because in my opinion I didn't do anything to them. I was just being me. And I wasn't about to act differently in order to try to please them. If I did, they'd probably find something new about me to dislike.

I might as well continue being me and have them like me or dislike me for who I really was.

I'd rather be genuine than a puppet with someone pulling my strings.

. . . At Eastside High School, a few paces in front of me, the captain of the basketball team had just bent close to the captain of the cheerleading squad and softly kissed her. Now he held her hand and walked with her among our teammates down the hallway.

He was handsome. And they looked sweet and beautiful and perfect.

Sometimes a male's attention toward a girl was nice.

My boyfriend, Benny, only ever touched me with warmth and teasing. I'd had precious little of that.

Suddenly, Benny appeared beside me with a smile. As usual, he playfully tugged my braid.

I rolled my eyes. "Now I know how the term 'freshman' probably originated. Cecelia!" I called to my friend. "Would you *please* get your cousin?"

Benny laughed.

That night he walked me home.

I let Benny kiss me. At first it felt a little uncomfortable, but then it became comfortable.

And then I saw stars.

7 A Soul Divided

Outside our living room window, the PSE&G representative turned off the electric and gas supplies to our house. Without a glance in our direction, he got into his van, made a note on his clipboard, and then drove away.

"Whose turn to go up the pole?"

One of my older male cousins was already heading out the front door.

My mother did the best she could with what she had for my cousins and brothers. But there were times when we had neither gas nor electricity because we didn't have enough money to pay for it. The electric and gas people from PSE&G came and turned them both off on a regular basis. My family members had learned how to climb up the tall brown electrical pole outside to illegally turn the electricity and gas back on, so we could have heat and hot water so that we could survive.

It felt awful to steal, especially with everything Mr. Clark was teaching my classmates and me about integrity, but sometimes this was just the way things were.

Even though I wasn't a high school sophomore yet, I began to look forward to college. Mr. Clark told us education was our homerun out of the ghetto, and indicated college was the grand slam and it had to lead to a better life than this.

My siblings, cousins and I worked and shared the household expenses with my mother. When we were old enough, we all worked for the Paterson CETA (The Comprehensive Employment and Training Act), a federally funded program that provided summer jobs, or we found other jobs to help out.

My oldest brother (God, rest his soul), he tried to do some positive things, but it seemed there was always money missing, and items kept being stolen by him or by other family members who lived with us.

Cousins, aunts, and uncles moved in for weeks or months on end, even though we struggled with hard financial times ourselves. My mother always tried to help others when she could—and even when she couldn't.

All of that made it very difficult to live in peace in my house.

Sometimes there was not enough food. We also ate a lot of government cheese sandwiches when my mother was able to get that rectangular box of government cheese.

Sometimes we were on welfare and received food stamps.

The summer following freshman year, I fell in love with my boyfriend, Benny, heart and soul.

Finally, I had someone to love me.

His mother became a second mom to me. She took me to church with her family, and Second Baptist Church became my church family.

Reverend Alexander McDonald III, a strong, God-fearing man, gave sermons that helped me grow as a young Christian.

I visited Benny's house nearly every day. Benny had an older sister and a younger brother who I loved dearly, and they treated me like family.

After church each week, I ate Sunday dinner with them in their home.

The first day of sophomore year, my friends and I walked up to Eastside School. The fences had been repaired or replaced, the grounds cleaned up, and the windows fixed and washed.

Inside we passed Mr. Clark and his bullhorn on our way to the auditorium (walking to the right!), and saw that colorful pictures had been added to the walls. As we approached the auditorium, we saw the trophy cases had been expanded. Their spotless shelves and sparkling glass proudly displayed the trophies won by our teams.

Our school was really starting to look good.

(EHS Trophy Case – Photo Courtesy EHS Yearbook, 1983)

After Mr. Clark took the stage and introduced himself to the freshmen, we sang the alma mater. Then he laid out the rules. He ended the list of regulations and consequences with, "Your education is your home run! Once you get it, no one can take it from you! But *you've* got to get it!"

After that he told us that a game room had been added to the school. He'd also bought radios for the cafeteria so that students could listen to music during lunch (and stay calm instead of start food fights, no doubt).

Then he said, "This year, we're implementing a new uniform policy! It's not mandatory, but you can participate if you choose to! Think about how much time you waste at home each morning before school trying to look good! Trying to look better than your classmates! You're trying to look fine with Sassoon on your behind, but you've got nothing in your mind! So wear a uniform! You can quit wasting all that time in the morning and make things easy for yourself! You can just wear your uniform and not worry about how you look! You can wear your uniform and show pride in your school!

"Student leaders and athletes, you can lead the show of pride by being the first to buy and wear the uniform!"

Thrilled with the idea, I wanted to be the first one to wear the uniform! Mr. Clark told us the price, which I knew my mother and I couldn't afford, then he told us if we wanted more information about it or had any questions, we could go to the office and talk to his secretary, Miss Hernandez.

When Mr. Clark dismissed us, I hurried straight to the office. I knocked on the door then walked in.

Miss Hernandez smiled. "Can I help you?"

"Yes. I'm Pinky. Can I leave a message for Mr. Clark?"

"What do you want to ask him? Maybe I can help."

"I'd like to wear the school uniform he just told us about. But my family doesn't have the money to pay for it." I wasn't embarrassed to tell her that. It's how things had always been.

She said, "Let me take down your name so I can give Mr. Clark your message. If you come back to the office at the end of the school day, I should have a reply for you."

That afternoon when I returned, Miss Hernandez said, "Pinky, I spoke to Mr. Clark. He said we're going to pay for your uniform. Now, you'll have a sweater, skirt, shirt and pants. What sizes are you?"

My expression must have broadcast my excitement, because she smiled too.

I became one of the first students to wear the EHS school uniform, though it fast became the popular trend.

When I wore it, I felt part of something new and something good. I had become part of Eastside, and I boldly wore my show of support for Mr. Clark.

My mother appreciated Mr. Clark for buying me the uniform. As someone who always tried to help others when she could, my mother respected that.

A few of my friends and I walked together to class.

Cecelia asked, "Did you see Mr. Clark with that baseball bat?"

"No," I said. "Why does he have a baseball bat?"

Benny overheard and joined us. "He's been getting death threats. Probably from students he kicked out of Eastside. He's letting everyone know he'll use the bat if he needs to. But mostly I think it's a show of force. Maybe even a status symbol."

That made sense. Thugs in the ghetto carried baseball bats for the same reason. Mr. Clark was speaking a language they would understand.

Cecelia giggled. "I heard that Mr. Clark said, 'Everyone used to call me Crazy Joe. Now they can call me Batman!'"

Benny said, "He's making sure whoever threatened him will hear about him carrying a bat."

"Well, it's a smart way to protect himself," I said.

A kid walking in front of us heard us and turned around. He wasn't wearing a school uniform. "I'd like to take Mr. Clark's bat and hit him with it, and then wrap it around his throat. Who does he think he is?"

Mr. Clark appeared in the hallway several classrooms down the corridor. The kid grunted in Mr. Clark's direction then turned into a classroom.

A student stopped Mr. Clark and asked him a question. Mr. Clark tucked the bullhorn under his arm, took some money out of his pocket, and gave it to the student along with a pat to the shoulder.

Then Mr. Clark continued down the hall, bullhorn to his mouth. "Everyone, walk to the right! Class is about to begin! Walk expeditiously to the right!"

Not long after sophomore year began, an amazing thing happened. I found a handwritten note in my locker from Ann—the girl I'd fought with about two years earlier at the pizza restaurant. Ann apologized to me for being cruel during elementary school.

"You never did anything bad to me; I was just following behind the other girls. I'm sorry for treating you the way I did."

After reading the note, I cried, because those girls didn't realize just how badly they'd hurt my feelings. They'd bullied me all through my middle school years. I thanked God that he'd made a strong little girl out of, because I could have allowed their cruelty to affect me in so many negative ways.

Ann and I met in the hallway a couple of days later, and we hugged.

She said, "I'm sorry!"

"I forgive you!"

Maybe she, and perhaps a few others, had realized that I'd simply chosen a different path than they had. I wasn't doing anything against them. I was just being me.

As one of the more outgoing kids, I was fairly popular, I was known for always wearing the color pink (my favorite color; I still wore it on days my Eastside uniform was in the laundry), and I participated in sports, choir, theater, cheerleading, yearbook and the dynamic Marching 100 band. I was the first female snare drummer.

(Pinky Miller, 1983 Cheerleader & 1985 Snare Drummer)

(Marching 100 Band - Courtesy of EHS Yearbook, 1985)

(Courtesy of EHS Yearbook, 1985, Pinky Miller second drummer on the left)

Civil rights icon Miss Rosa Parks came to visit Eastside High School! Since I had home economics class, I helped cook lunch for Miss Parks and the many dignitaries who accompanied her. To be able to serve her was *awesome*!!!

(Civil Rights Icon – Rosa Parks being served lunch by students – Pinky Miller on far left, Derrick McDuffie, Gwen Melvin, Mr. Clark – Photo Courtesy of Pinky Miller)

During my sophomore year we went to visit Howard University located in Washington, DC. We stayed overnight with some of the college students. I fortunately stayed with some of the ladies of Alpha Kappa Alpha Sorority Inc. They were very nice to me and the other young ladies that were with me. They began to tell us stories about their college experiences and gave us some words of wisdom of what not to do as a young lady and the importance of furthering our education. They exclaimed "Getting your education is a serious matter!" "When you come to school be careful not to get a bad reputation and go to class!" "Get involved in extra-curricular activities and have fun!" We had a great time and ever since I was 15 years old I knew that I was going to become a member of Alpha Kappa Alpha Sorority Incorporated.

Sometimes, things get better and better!

When I was fifteen, I encountered my father's daughter. I met my sister!

My second eldest cousin, Zaya, lived in Paterson in an apartment building that was set aside for people whose career was in the arts. My cousin's profession was hair braiding and modeling. She was also a very good in-home decorator and had added pictures of our family members to the walls of her home.

As Zaya braided the hair of a new client in her living room, she realized something familiar about her.

Zaya said, "You look like somebody I know. I can't put my finger on it, but you really look like someone I know!"

Puzzled, Zaya continued to braid her client's hair. As she did, she looked at the pictures of her cousins that hung on the walls. Her eyes stopped on the picture of me.

Zaya looked back and forth between the picture of me and her client. "I got it! I found it! You look like my baby cousin! You look like my baby cousin!"

The client asked, "May I see the picture of your cousin?"

Zaya pulled my picture off her wall and handed it to her client.

They both stared at the picture and realized there was a strong resemblance.

Her client said, "Amazing. We do look alike."

The two discussed things and started to put some pieces together. They realized that her client and I possibly shared the same father.

After Zaya finished the braiding, she noticed her client was upset.

Her client paid then abruptly left my cousin's apartment.

The client lived in the same apartment building because her husband played an instrument in a band. Her husband and Zaya knew each other well.

Zaya continued this conversation with her client's husband.

He said, "My wife is very upset and very much in denial. She said, 'My father would never do something like that! That's not my sister!'"

As a result, that relationship was tarnished and my cousin never braided the woman's hair again.

Zaya told me what had happened.

A couple of months later, I went to visit Zaya. As I entered the apartment building, a young woman was walking out. Looking at her was almost like looking into a mirror at myself.

She stared at me (in a not so very nice tone), and I stared at her, then we passed each other. Each had realized who the other was.

I was so excited, I ran upstairs and told Zaya. "I just saw my other sister, even though she didn't appear to be very happy about it!" *I* was happy and said, "Maybe I'll get to meet my other family someday!"

Already I was looking forward to it.

Like my mother, I loved being active. In addition to my school-based activities, I participated in fashion shows as a model, and won modeling competitions for the Distributive Education Clubs of America (DECA).

The Paterson Task Force created the Miss Paterson pageant, and I participated in the very first one in 1984.

In the school cafeteria, Mr. Clark and his bullhorn made the rounds, pausing to talk with students or to have them recite or sing the alma mater. When he approached the table I shared with my friends, I stood up. "Mr. Clark?"

"Yes, Pinky, what do you need?"

"I'm in the pageant running for Miss Paterson 1984."

"That's great. Good job."

"Well, I have to raise money for the pageant. Would you be willing to buy a booster or an ad for the pageant booklet?"

"Sure, just go to the office."

"Thank you, Mr. Clark!"

In the office, Miss Hernandez smiled. "Hello, Pinky. What can I do for you?"

I explained about the pageant. "Mr. Clark said that he would help support me with an ad in the pageant booklet."

"What do we need to do?"

I gave her a form. "Would you be able to fill this out and let me know what page size you want the ad to be?"

"Of course. I'll connect with Mr. Clark and get it done."

Mr. Clark helped us kids whenever he could.

The evening of the Miss Paterson pageant, I was excited to be named second runner-up.

When I was fifteen, I lost my virginity with Benny. I know now that it was only by the grace of God that I didn't get pregnant, because we had sex on a regular basis without any protection. Benny also introduced me to pornography. We used to watch it on cable television at his house after dark on Saturday nights.

Only in the distant, hazy corners of my mind did it occur to me that sex at an early age was precisely the choice that my mother and my grandmother had made, the choice that had forced each of them to accept unwanted marriages, abusive relationships, unfulfilled love, and decades of poverty, stress, and hardship while they raised multiple children alone.

During the two years I'd had a relationship with Benny, Mr. Clark specifically told me, many times, "Leave that boy alone!"

But I just knew I was head over heels in love with Benny.

Yet Mr. Clark told me, "Pinky! Stay in your books and leave those boys alone!"

Too late. I realized he was right about those boys.

Benny cheated on me with an upper classmate who just wanted to see if she could get him into bed with her, and she did.

It broke my heart. I cried for days. The pain felt unbearable!

After she dumped him, he tried to get back with me many times. My heart would not allow me to go through that pain again.

As a result of that heartache, I decided not to date or deal with any more high school boys. I was too mature for them, and they were stupid!

For months I listened to the radio a lot and cried myself to sleep listening to sad love songs.

During those days at Eastside, Mr. Clark taught me that I did not have to lower my standards for boys. He taught me that education was important, that discipline was important, and that God was very important. "God loves you," he said, "and so do I!"

Mr. Clark helped me to refocus my attention on what mattered, and what would endure.

Mr. Clark also taught me that if I wanted something I could go after it, and no one could stop me, with the exception of me.

When he saw me looking listless or sad in the hallway or cafeteria, he said, "Pinky! I know you can do it! Just keep striving!"

Mr. Clark was, in my eyes, my father.

When my friends and I strode into Eastside in 1984 to begin our junior year, we saw that plants and couches now dotted the hallways. These were places where students could hang out and relax between classes or during cafeteria time.

They weren't the only discovery I made my junior year.

I'm not certain why, but I was only attracted to light-skinned boys. I didn't date anyone, but I thought a number of the light-skinned boys were good looking.

While working at Toys "R" Us, I met a handsome coworker, a very nice guy, who attended the other high school in Paterson and had plans to go to college. He bought me lunch sometimes, and thoughtful little gifts, and we occasionally went to the movies.

But he was also a dark-skinned brother, and I could not see myself with him because of the color of his skin.

He wanted to date me. Frequently he asked me why he couldn't be my boyfriend. I gave some lame excuse for fear of hurting his feelings.

One day he kept asking me.

I said, "Your skin is too dark." Then I saw his bright, beautiful smile turn fade into a frown of sadness.

I don't know why that happened, why I was struck with colorism, and I don't know why I was so attracted to light-skinned men. However, being rejected by my biological father was a constant ache in my heart, and my father was a dark-skinned man.

I told my friend, "I am so sorry! I know it's wrong! I am so sorry!" I hurt his feelings, and it was terribly wrong of me. The color of one's skin doesn't determine a person's character or how they will treat you, and he was a good, good person.

My own bias had just cost me a treasured friend.

Near the end of my junior year in 1985, I participated again in the Miss Paterson pageant. As before, Mr. Clark supported me in the pageant by purchasing an ad for the program booklet.

During the final event, I was named first runner-up.

Shortly before high school graduation in 1986, I participated in the Miss Paterson pageant one last time. Mr. Clark loyally purchased another ad for the pageant program to support me.

For the modeling and question-and-answer portion of the contest, my cousin, Leah, allowed me to wear her beautiful wedding dress.

For my talent, I reenacted the juke joint scene from the movie *The Color Purple*, which had just debuted, when Shug Avery sang the song "Miss Celie's Blues." I set up a table and a life-sized brown manikin that I'd dressed in a big brown hat and clothes like Celie in the movie. I wore a tight-fitting red dress very much like Shug Avery's, complete with the feathers, beads, sequins, and high heels. I sang and performed the song just like the character in the movie.

I won the pageant!

(Miss Paterson Pageant Trophies – Left - 2nd Runner-up 1984, Center – Winner-1986, Right-1st Runner-up)

(Photos Courtesy of Pinky Miller)

Mr. Clark had been right with everything he taught us! "Go after what you want, and don't let fear hold you back. Persistence will overcome resistance!"

(Mr. Joe Clark & Pinky Miller, 1986)

Graduation day!

The class of 1986 was the 100th graduating class as displayed on the commencement invitation of Eastside High School.

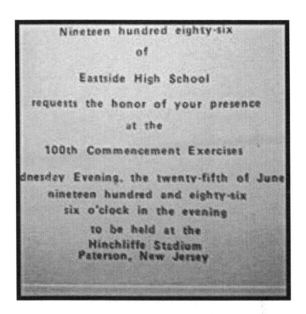

Nineteen hundred eighty-six
of
Eastside High School
requests the honor of your presence
at the
100th Commencement Exercises
dnesday Evening, the twenty-fifth of June
nineteen hundred and eighty-six
six o'clock in the evening
to be held at the
Hinchliffe Stadium
Paterson, New Jersey

Olandha Seldon

(Olandha "Pinky" Seldon)

It finally came, and it was filled with laughter and tears of joy.

Our graduation took place at the famous Hinchliffe Stadium. Mr. Clark gave a resounding, uplifting speech to his first graduating class—the class of 1986!

Mr. Clark gave us our wings to fly, and told us to make him proud.

(Photo Courtesy of EHS Yearbook, 1989)

The empty halls of Eastside High echoed with the sound of my summer flip-flops. At the office I knocked on the door then walked inside. Miss Hernandez smiled at me, like always.

"Pinky, school's out! What are you doing here?"

"It's good to see you, Miss Hernandez. I wanted to say hi to Mr. Clark if he's in."

"Just a moment. I'll see if he's available."

She disappeared into his office and then reappeared with Mr. Clark beside her.

"Hi, Pinky!"

"Hi, Mr. Clark. I wanted to thank you for supporting me in the Miss Paterson pageant and show you my crown."

"Well let's see it!"

I lifted the crown out of my pink shoulder bag and set it on my head. I also handed him a souvenir pageant program booklet.

"It's very nice," he said. "Congratulations! What school are you going to?"

"I'm going to Montclair State University."

"That's great. Make sure you do us proud!"

"I will." I gave him a hug and told him and Miss Hernandez goodbye.

It felt good to have walked in the front doors and still received genuine interest and love from them. Happy-sad tears pricked my nose. I was going to really miss these people.

Outside the office in the corridor, after tucking the crown back into my shoulder bag, I began the walk toward the entrance doors.

Mr. Clark had instilled in us a better way of thinking about ourselves and our communities. My high school days had inspired me in ways I'd never thought possible when my friend Jackie and I first approached Eastside as scared young freshmen four years before.

Eastside, which at one point I'd thought looked like a prison, had been a safe haven for so many of us. A fortress. Mr. Clark had made sure that happened for all the students. Because of it, we'd been free to learn.

Now, four years later, Eastside's floors sparkled with fresh polish. Sofas and plants stood along walls alive with rich paintings and colorful murals created by former graffiti artists.

"EASTSIDE"

(Photos Courtesy of EHS Yearbook, 1988)

Like a caterpillar in its chrysalis, Eastside had been transformed, and the students had transformed along with it.

Mr. Clark had shared his knowledge, his vision, and his love, and we, his students, would be able to succeed because of him.

I was going to miss Mr. Clark's loud voice through the bullhorn. I was going to miss his word of the day. I was going to miss singing the alma mater.

I was just going to miss my high school days, because I'd had fun, and they'd turned out to be some of the best days of my life.

The changes Mr. Clark implemented at Eastside made national news. Famous people regularly visited Eastside to talk with and inspire the students, including:

- New Jersey Governor Thomas Kean
- Mayor Frank Graves
- Dr. Frank Napier, Superintendent of Paterson Public Schools
- Dr. Gwendolyn Goldsby Grant, educator, lecturer, author
- Rosa Parks, civil rights icon
- Yolanda King, civil rights activist, daughter of Dr. Martin Luther King Jr.
- Atallah Shabazz, civil rights activist, daughter of Malcolm X
- Ralph Carter, actor in *Good Times* sitcom
- Chris Rock, comedian
- Run DMC, rap group
- New Edition, R&B artists
- The Winans, gospel music group
- Rory Sparrow, professional basketball player, Eastside alum
- Curtis Sliwa, founder of the Guardian Angels
- Morton Downey Jr., famous talk show host

In addition, Mr. Clark received a telephone call from President of the United States Ronald Reagan, congratulating him on a job well done.

But Mr. Clark didn't receive such recognition by always following the rules.

Despite everything Mr. Clark had done for us, his first graduating class, he got into a lot of trouble fighting for his students because he didn't always adhere to regulations set forth by the Paterson Board of Education.

After my class graduated, filming began for the movie *Lean on Me*. The movie would dramatically chronicle the radical changes Mr. Clark made at Eastside High, and the difference he made for the students as both a tough, no-nonsense principal and a father figure who cared deeply about the kids.

Some educators and members of the Board of Education were not happy with how the movie portrayed the students. Audiences, however, experienced something more: hope that one principal's conviction and uncompromising approach would create waves of change in challenged public schools across the nation.

The movie grossed more than thirty-one million dollars in 1989.

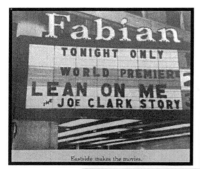 

(Courtesy of EHS Yearbook, 1989, *Lean on Me* Gala - Courtesy of EHS Yearbook, 1989)

Soon after the movie was released, Mr. Clark left Eastside and went on the lecture circuit.

COLLEGE!

During the summer of 1986, I started attending Montclair State University, thrilled to be admitted to the health careers program—a program for students who wanted to excel in the sciences and math to become doctors.

I was admitted to the program because I wanted to be a dentist. In high school I'd had many dreams of becoming a dentist, actress, model, and/or the next Oprah Winfrey. At the moment, dentistry held the greatest appeal.

That summer I lived on campus in Freeman Hall, and I had a blast! Of our group of about thirty students, I was the only one with a car. So whenever we needed to get off campus, my car was the way out. We took classes during the day, studied during the late afternoon, then the evenings were ours. I soon met many different people from so many different walks of life, and my college life had just begun!

I was involved with the Black Student Cooperative Union, the modeling/fashion show group, the gospel choir, and student government association.

I was also a desk assistant and was very active within my residence hall. My friends and I hung out and went to dance clubs, like the Cheetah Club and Club 88. We had a ball dancing to house music all night until the sun came up.

Although I was very active in college and had a lot of fun, I'd been ill-prepared for college academically. In order to be able to compete with my classmates, I had to take a number of remedial courses. I did not allow that to stop me from gaining as much education as I possibly could, and I owed a lot of that determination to my mother and to Mr. Clark, who'd instilled in me to never give up and to keep pushing forward for the things that I want in life.

The Black Student Cooperative Union was an organization of African American and other minority students who wanted to provide programs and activities for students of color campus wide. The organization was funded by student activities fees and provided leadership opportunities for students who wanted to be involved.

I started out as a member of the organization. By my second year, I was the vice president. By my third year, I was president of the organization. As such, I was able to build my leadership skills as well as hold administrators and faculty accountable to assist students of color in any way needed, especially when it came to racial issues.

This phenomenal organization also provided financial assistance, food, parties, and gospel concerts (which I directed!) for the students at Montclair State University. Becoming a member of Alpha Kappa Alpha Sorority Incorporated was an awesome goal that I was fortunate enough to attain as well. My leadership skills increased tremendously, and I made several lifelong friends that I still cherish today. Selena Robinson, Sharon Hargraves, Charlotte Cade and Genevieve Hardy are my friends for life.

As my freshman year in college progressed, I increasingly discussed family matters with my roommate and other students. I became aware of what positive familial relationships could and should be like.

My home life, I realized, had been less than desirable, compared to the childhoods of many other students.

I decided to write a letter to my mother. In it I revealed to her some of my experiences as a child, many things that she had been unaware of because she had been away working much of the time.

I shared many personal issues with her, including my disappointment in how she'd handled my introduction to my father at the bowling alley when I was ten, and how she'd yelled at me in the car afterward for not handling an adult situation well as a child.

I also shared with her my dismay that she hadn't held my sperm donor accountable for his responsibilities as a father.

The letter probably hurt her feelings. There's no question she tried to do the best she knew how to do.

But I was angry with my mother for many years, because she had not protected me the way she should have.

Excerpt from my diary—Friday, January 23, 1987—age 18

Today was not a pleasant day. I had a very strong urge to speak to my so-called father. I called! I spoke to him to tell him that the situation with my sister, his daughter who lives in my other cousin's building, is really starting to bother me. He and she both deny that he is my father.

When I spoke to him, he acted as if he didn't know what I was talking about.

He hurt my feelings really bad. I felt so hurt. I sat and cried like a baby.

It bothers me not to know for certain who my father is. My mother and Donald told me that Olin was, but Olin flatly denies it. And yet I look just one of his daughters. It just hurts not being accepted!

I prayed and asked God to help make things better. He impressed upon me to leave it all in God's hands. And that's just what I plan to do. Thank you, Jesus!

I stayed home all day.

Excerpt from my diary—Saturday, February 21, 1987

Today was so much fun! Rho fraternity was having a party up at Montclair State tonight, so the campus was filled with nothing but Rho fraternity brothers! Those brothers look good! They were all on our dorm floor having a brunch. I was walking up and down the hallway buggin' (having fun, laughing) out with some friends. I saw Rob, and he introduced me to his frat brothers. It was nice.

Later on when I was cooking some ravioli in the lounge/kitchenette, one of his fraternity brothers started buggin' me out. He walked into the lounge and sat down on the couch and asked, "What are you cooking?"

"Ravioli."

"Can I have some?"

"No."

"Why not?"

I managed not to laugh. "Because I don't know you and I only have this one can of ravioli!"

"My name is Bob Barnes Jr! Now can I have some of your ravioli?"

We just laughed and began to have a conversation. He is a nice-looking guy, and is very interesting. He's twenty-five years old, works two full-time jobs, drives a 1987 Nissan Maxima, and overall it seems as though we're compatible. I felt real comfortable around him.

He asked, "Would you like to go to the party with me?"

I said, "Sure."

Later on we went to his fraternity party. I wore my gold two-piece outfit. Yes, it was definitely working! We danced together all night. Afterward we went to breakfast then came back to the dorm. He stayed overnight; we talked until about 6:30 this morning. We were buggin', and it was fun.

We exchanged phone numbers and other contact information, and told each other we would stay in touch.

A couple of days after I met Bob, on February 26, 1987, I received a letter from him telling me that it had been very nice to meet me and that he really liked me a lot. He asked me to write him a letter to tell him where my head was right then.

I'd just met the man five days ago, and I didn't know where my head was about anything. I wrote the letter and let him know that it was also very nice to meet him and that we'd see where things went from there.

My get-togethers with Bob turned into a relationship very quickly. I was no longer dating other guys and he was no longer dating other girls. We soon became sexually active and met each other's families. My family liked Bob a lot, and his family liked me a lot.

Bob was really concerned about my education and wanted to make sure that I stayed focused on obtaining good grades. We wrote each other letters often, and he came from Ossining, New York, to visit me in New Jersey every week. He'd spend the night in my dorm room, and we'd go to church on Sunday. He got to know my college friends very well.

We fell in love with each other and were in a committed relationship. Bob frequently took me to Red Lobster, my favorite seafood restaurant, and we went to concerts and movies and dinner dates just about every week.

Bob was also concerned about my spending habits and tried to help me lower my credit card debt and to stop spending money.

Bob invited me to go with him to Canada to see Niagara Falls for my spring break. I was very surprised and excited. No one had ever taken me anywhere like that before! I was elated that I was going on a plane to another country and that I was about to experience something new with someone I loved.

Near the end of my first year in college, I decided to write a letter to my father and his wife. As far as I knew, she knew nothing of my existence.

That letter had to have hurt her feelings. I didn't mean to intentionally hurt her. I just wanted and needed to be recognized by my father. I wanted and needed to have a relationship with him. To receive a letter in the mail, to find out that your husband had had an affair nineteen years ago and you, as the nurse, most likely held that baby not realizing it was the seed of your husband, would be a hard pill to swallow.

Basically in the letter, I introduced myself to them. I shared with them all the positive things happening in my life—college, I'd recently won the Miss Paterson 1986 pageant, I had done very well in high school, and I was outgoing and active in a positive way.

I also shared with his wife how I came to be, at least from my mother's side of the story.

Then I shared with them that was I coming to their house for a visit soon. However, I didn't put a date on when I was going to visit.

I mailed the letter and began to plan my journey to see my long lost father.

Bob and I dated for the rest of the semester. Before the semester ended, Bob asked me if I would go to the Aruba with him for five days.

Of course, I said yes!

It was beautiful, and we had a terrific time. We went swimming in the ocean, took tons of pictures, and met lots of new people. It was the trip of a lifetime.

That summer I stayed some weeks with him at his mother's house, and at my mother's house. Our relationship started to get really serious, and we talked about marriage, children, and our future goals.

Before the end of summer, I headed back to school early because I was accepted to be a resident assistant for the upcoming year. I was going to start RA training.

Despite the old saying, what goes around doesn't always come around.

My mother said she was told by a relative that Aunt Eva, who'd horrifically abused my mother and her brother when they were children, was ill and not doing well. After searching several hospitals and nursing homes, my mother found Aunt Eva in New York, living in a nursing home unfit for elderly people to live in.

Aunt Eva had been placed there at the age of seventy-nine. Her husband, a minister, had taken all of her possessions, and the state of New York had sold her abandoned home. The state gave half of the funds to her estranged husband. The other half they gave to the nursing home.

She was homeless and didn't have anyone to take care of her.

My mother told me, "When I saw her sitting aimless and sick in that wheelchair, all the anger went away from me, and I forgave her! God did that! I've brought her to New Jersey to live with us."

(My mother took care of Aunt Eva until the woman died at the age of eighty-nine. My mother provided for her and was her caregiver for those ten years. Not many people would have done the same. I trust Aunt Eva had been deeply thankful to God for inspiring my mother to forgive her.)

Excerpt from my diary—Wednesday, August 12, 1987

Guess what? This is the happiest day of my life thus far! My baby proposed to me!!!

It started out as a regular day. I was at his house resting from this drastic hard-working summer. Then there was a call on the phone—it was Bob. He asked me to get dressed because we were going to go out for dinner.

We went to our favorite place—where else except Red Lobster? After we both got the sampler platter as usual, we talked and were buggin' out.

He'd told me earlier that he was going to the city, but he hadn't said why. Now I asked, and he said "fraternity business." After dinner, we went over to the arcade where I played my favorite arcade game, Millipede, and he played Turbo. When I ran out of playing money, I asked him for some quarters. He ignored me and kept his concentration on his game. You know me—I started to dig in his pockets.

There were no quarters in any of his pants pockets, so I went to the jacket. The first pocket didn't have anything in it, so I went to the second.

I stuck my hand in and, wow, I felt a box—a jewelry box.

I was so scared, I just dropped the box back in his pocket. I thought, "Oh, my God!!! That can't be what I think it is?" I started getting a little nervous and started buggin' out.

We'd talked about marriage before, but suddenly he looked at me, stopped playing his game, and said to me, "You spoil everything!"

I hugged and kissed him, then we headed outside and went for a walk. All at once I started crying. I finally, really realized that someone truly loved me.

I just couldn't get over it. I could not stop crying. I cried and cried, and he hugged me and kissed me and asked, "Why are you crying?"

I said, "Because I love you and I'm very happy!"

As I kept crying, he took my hand and said, "I want to ask you something. Pinky, what are your plans for next summer?"

That just made me cry even more.

He asked me, "Are we down?"

Crying, I said, "Yes."

Then, as he slipped the ring onto my finger, he asked me, "Will you marry me?"

I said, "Yes! Yes!"

I cried so much, so much, that after about two hours he said, "If I knew you were going to cry this much, I wouldn't have given it to you."

I said, "What?" and we started to laugh.

After a while, when we were riding in his car, I was still crying and looking at this gorgeous thirteen-diamond one-carat gold ring. I thought I would die. It sparkled so much.

We stopped at 7-Eleven. He bought me something in a bag—all of a sudden he pulled out a rose. It just made me cry more. I kissed him and said, "Thank you!"

I thanked God so much—it was just so happy and wonderful.

Thank you, Jesus, for bringing Bob Barnes Junior into my life!

Despite the emotional extremes I'd experienced over the past few years, and the times I'd thought my soul would split somewhere between the thrills and the heartbreaks, God had only been preparing me for what was yet to come.

8 Standing Up

I prepared for my journey to see my long lost father.

My childhood friend, Cecelia, had moved to St. Louis, Missouri, during high school. I contacted her to see if I could visit her, and to see if she would go with me to see my father. She agreed, and I planned the trip.

On a warm August day, my plane touched down in St. Louis, Missouri.

Cecelia and I rented a car, bought an atlas, and began the four-hour drive to Joplin, Missouri. As we talked, I shared with her what I hoped would happen that day. My prayer was to be welcomed with open arms and a smile.

After being lost for some time, we finally found the address.

I drove up and parked the car on the street in front of a very nice house. Its lush, green lawn looked carefully tended, and its front door both charmed and welcomed.

I felt nervous and excited all at once!

Cecelia and I walked up to the house. I rang the bell.

A short, dark-skinned man opened the door.

A big smile filled my face, because I now knew that this was my father.

Excited, I said, "Hello!"

He barked, "Get in here, with all the trouble you caused!"

Then he turned and sat down inside on a staircase. He stared at me like he saw a ghost or something.

I thought, *This is weird*, and my big Kool-Aid smile disappeared.

I'd hoped for a hug, or something, but not this type of welcome.

After several moments, I began to sense significant tension throughout the house. It felt like an evil spirit filled the place.

Cecelia and I walked inside. The stairs ascended from a plush looking living room. We went and sat on the couch.

I asked, "Why were you not in my life?"

My father's panicked eyes had followed my movements, but he remained mute.

Suddenly a woman strode into the room, and snarled, "Girl, you need to go back to where you came from, because you are not getting any money from him!"

Within seconds, I became surprised, confused, hurt, sad, and then very mad!

As tears began to roll down my face, I said to this woman, his wife, "First of all, I am not here for any money! I came here to meet my father and have a relationship with him!"

His wife I began to have a strong exchange of words.

I said, "You should understand, as a mother! I grew up without a father! I did not ask to come here, but I am here! All I want to do is have a relationship with my father!"

She said, "Whoever's been taking care of you, will have to continue taking care of you, because you're not getting any money!"

I was upset and angry and crying. Unable to get through to either of them, we walked out. Still my father said nothing, even though he watched us go.

As I drove back toward St. Louis, I shook with emotion. That had not been the reception I had prayed for.

Now I just wanted to get out of the misery—and Missouri—as soon as possible.

A police siren broke into my mental replays of the visit. The police pulled me over for driving 102 mph in a 70 mph zone. They actually took me to the police station and ordered me to pay a ticket of $400 before they would release me. I called Bob and explained to him that I needed the money so that I wouldn't be put in jail. Being the kind boyfriend that he was, he paid the ticket.

Finally Cecelia and I resumed driving. In St. Louis, I thanked Cecelia, got on an airplane, and headed home to New Jersey.

To say I was hurt, would be an understatement. I was nineteen, yet I felt ten all over again.

It had also hurt to see that my father and his wife lived what appeared to be a very plush lifestyle. My mother had to struggle with raising six kids by herself, and my father hadn't sent one red cent or ever lent a hand to help raise me.

However, a single ray of sunshine broke through my gloom as I recalled one very endearing fact: I looked like my father.

Excerpt from my diary—Sunday, August 16, 1987

This past weekend I went to Missouri. I saw Cecelia, and we went to see my father. What a great day. Yes, it was definitely a blessing, yet hurtful at the same time.

I must carry out plan B for my father, Mr. Olin, whatever that may be. Not quite sure what to do next.

During the four years I lived on campus at Montclair State University, I discovered the difference between a dorm and a residence hall: A dorm is a Dreary Old Room of Mine—a place where you eat and sleep. On the other hand, a residence hall is a place where you eat, sleep, learn, and grow.

When I was selected as a resident assistant, which was one of the top leadership positions on campus, I was overjoyed because I liked to help people with their problems.

A resident assistant serves as a counselor, friend, disciplinarian, or referral agent.

We RA's trained for two weeks prior to the new freshmen coming to campus. The training was to prepare the resident assistants to be able to help the residents in any way to help make sure that they would be successful inside and outside of the classroom.

Training included conflict resolution, safety, health issues, relationship concerns, race relations, diversity, leadership, emergency protocols, programming, team building, along with regulations, policies, and preparation for the upcoming year.

The day before the new students were scheduled to arrive on campus, an additional set of student leaders arrived early. They were called OWLs—Orientation Workshop Leaders. They would help the new students with orientation to Montclair State University.

Some of the orientation workshop leaders lived on my floor in Bohn Hall and were working hard to prepare for the next day's freshman orientation. Many of us were up late getting everything set up for check-in the following day, by doing room checks, maintenance reports, door decorations, bulletin boards, and getting the building ready for opening day.

We all went to sleep after midnight.

At about three o'clock in the morning, I awoke to fists banging frantically on my door.

In the hall, several women screamed, "You need to come down to the lobby! Someone is hurt!"

I fumbled for my glasses, hurried out, then ran with the students down the hallway to where a larger group paced and cried. At their feet, a student lay on the floor. Both she and the floor around her were covered with streams of blood.

She'd cut her wrist in an attempt to commit suicide. It looked like she was on the verge of succeeding.

I teetered on the verge of an out-of-body experience. This was the first time I experienced such a serious life threatening situation that included so much blood.

I looked over into her room. Blood streaked the walls.

On the inside I wanted to bust out in tears, scream, and act just as frantic as the others. However, I prayed, and God calmed me down from the inside out.

I ran to the emergency phone, called 911, and called my hall director and the emergency staff person on duty.

Then I knelt next to the bleeding student, speaking softly to her and keeping her awake.

Within minutes the professionals arrived and took over the situation.

During those two hours before sunrise, I fully realized that the position I had as a resident assistant was not to be taken lightly. I was responsible for the students' lives and well-being.

Thankfully, the student lived.

After the event was over, I returned to my room and cried and trembled from the stress of what had happened. How true it was that we are our brothers' and sisters' keeper. It's up to us to stand up and make a difference.

My fiancé, Bob, constantly pressed me to set a date for us to marry. I always replied, "I don't know when, but not now!" As a college student finishing up my sophomore year, I had goals I needed to achieve before even thinking about setting a date.

Did I love him? Yes.

Did he love me? Yes.

Did I truly understand what love was? No! I thought it was a wonderful emotion, one strong and enduring, like a sun that would never burn out.

In truth, the emotion of love is more like a light bulb. When it burns out, it's what you have left that enables a marriage to endure.

Marriage vows themselves do not refer to love as an emotion—a noun. They refer to love as an action—a verb. "Do you promise *to love. . . ?*" doesn't mean to feel love for. It means to show love, too.

At the age of nineteen, I was clueless about that and about the seriousness of marriage. All I knew was that someone finally loved me, paid attention to me, and wanted to be with me. Even so, I wasn't in a rush to walk down the aisle.

I felt pressured to set a date for the wedding. Accepting Bob's proposal to get married did not mean I wanted to get married within the next twelve months.

As the semester continued, I took classes, was vice president of the Black Student Cooperative Union, a resident assistant, a director of the gospel choir, and had a job on campus. I loved college life, and getting married was the furthest thing from my mind.

The topic of setting a date to wed grew into an ongoing debate.

Finally, Mr. Bob Barnes said, "Pinky, you can do all of those things you want and still get married. I don't care about you not living with me right now. I just want to marry you, and I'm willing to make sure you get to do everything you want to do."

I reluctantly agreed to set a date—June 18, 1988.

After careful evaluation of my academic strengths, I switched my major from health careers and the desire to become a dentist to communication studies. I took broadcasting classes because I wanted to either be the next Oprah, or work in a student affairs profession and continue to help students.

Planning the wedding was fun, for the most part. I chose one of my best friends from elementary school, Cassey, to be my maid of honor.

My family warned against my choosing Cassey. They thought of her as fast-tailed because she dated and had sex with my older brother during high school. But I didn't think of Cassey like that, and I told my family so.

My mother and my sister stressed to me that I needed to watch out for her. They said they had seen her looking at my fiancé as if she wanted him. I chose not to listen to their viewpoint. Cassey was my friend.

I chose my sister and cousins to be my bridesmaids and some additional friends as well. Bob's fraternity brothers were his groomsman.

To save money, I asked my aunt, a seamstress, to make the bridesmaids dresses as well as my wedding gown. She did a fair enough job with the bridesmaids' dresses. But on the morning of my wedding when I went to my aunt's house to try on my gown, it lay around her sewing room in several pieces, incomplete!

Half crazed, I drove through early morning traffic from Paterson to Willow Brook Mall in Wayne, New Jersey, eight miles away. In the mall's empty parking lot, I cried hysterically. The mall wouldn't open until ten.

I was getting married at four o'clock that afternoon.

I sat outside of the mall in my car, sobbing.

When the mall opened, I ran into JC Penney and headed straight for wedding/bridal area. Two women asked me if they could help me. I burst out crying even harder. "I'm supposed to get married today at four o'clock, and my aunt hasn't begun to sew together my gown!"

They shifted into professional-frantic mode and tried every gown on me they could find that might possibly fit.

Thank God for those two women, because they found a gown, even though it was a little big. Nonetheless, I bought it and left.

For some people, this predicament may have been a sign not to get married. For others it signified that love could conquer all.

Only time would tell which mine would be.

Our wedding was the talk of the town because a horse and buggy picked me up from my mother's house and drove me through Paterson. The buggy took me past Eastside High School and deposited me near Paterson Falls, where our ceremony would be. It was beautiful, a sight to see.

(Paterson, Falls - Photo Courtesy of Dr. Pinky Miller)

I wished my father could have been there.

That summer, 1988, became a full-out adventure! We moved to an apartment in Tarrytown, New York, that was affiliated with Bob's night job (he worked with emotionally disturbed children at night), and he worked his full-time job during the day. In essence, Bob was a workaholic. But we had fun and we learned a lot about each other, because this was the first time we had ever lived together.

In August, after two months of married life, I headed back to school to live on campus.

My junior year in college got underway, and I worked to be the best student and resident assistant I knew how. Bob had off work Wednesday nights and weekends, so we basically had a Wednesday-weekend marriage my junior year.

In June 1989, I went home to live with my husband for part of the summer. While there, I experienced symptoms of being pregnant. I had never been pregnant before, and I was ecstatic.

I paid a visit to the doctor, and they confirmed the pregnancy.

I couldn't wait to get home and tell Bob the news.

"A baby?" he said. "Pinky, I'm not ready to have a baby! There are other things I want to do before having kids. Why ever did you think I'd be happy about this? You'll have to get an abortion."

His words crushed my heart.

How dare you tell your wife—or even ask your wife—to get an abortion because you're not ready to have a child yet. Dammit! I hadn't been ready to get married! But there I stood, wedding band and all.

This argument was a major turning point for me. It hurt my heart so much that I became depressed and wanted to leave him.

But where could I go? Who wanted to be with a pregnant twenty-year-old?

I went to live on campus and took classes for the rest of the summer.

Our relationship continued to plummet, because he kept insisting I abort the baby.

I was going to keep my baby.

While on campus I continued to undertake leadership positions, and this started my third year as a resident assistant.

My college friends took good care of me and made sure my pregnancy was a positive one. They even gave me a baby shower.

At the end of the semester, in December, I had to leave campus. I went home to a man whom I'd lived with for less than four months, though we'd now been married for almost two years.

During my time at home with my husband, he made jokes and called me names pertaining to the weight I'd gain. He often called me fat and sometimes even called me a whale.

This was very hard for me because my family and friends lived in New Jersey, and I lived in New York, with a man I hardly knew, who verbally abused me while I was pregnant.

With his two full-time jobs, he rarely ventured home, so I spent a lot of time by myself.

One evening my telephone rang. The caller, an old girlfriend—
"god sister"—of Bob, and I struck up a conversation. I'd met her
once or twice before. We chatted about the new baby coming, and
I invited her over to see our new place.

She said, "Oh I've seen your apartment already."

I said, "What?"

"Bob has brought me over to the apartment."

Brief minutes later, I hung up the phone and called Bob. When
I asked him about it, he lied.

"Bob, I just spoke to her. She described our apartment."

He then tried to clean up the lie.

I'd had suspicions of Bob cheating on me with his other old
girlfriend, Darby, who used to work with him. And now he was
bringing women to our apartment and then lying about it.

At home, we got into a major argument, and he shoved me—
while I was pregnant! He could have harmed me and his unborn
child!

That evening I called one of my cousins and told her that he'd
shoved me. She basically said "get over it!" I was angry with her
for a very long time after that. As if I should accept abuse.

When she and I talked again, she explained that sometimes
things like that happened in marriages. I still did not accept it! A
man should *never* hit a woman, especially a pregnant woman!

When my delivery date of February 26, 1990 approached, my
doctor observed the dilation. He calculated that I would likely give
birth on my due date. With this being my first pregnancy and not
knowing what could happen, I asked Bob if he could stay home
with me around the due date, just in case I went into labor.

He went to both of his jobs.

On February 25th around midnight, I stepped out of the shower
and walked toward the bedroom.

A pain hit me so hard that it knocked me down to my knees.

I screamed from it as I crawled to the phone to notify the doctor. My contractions struck every four minutes apart. The doctor told me to come to the hospital.

I couldn't get up off the floor. I was naked and couldn't dress myself because the pain was excruciating. I called Bob, then I phoned my mother and cousin to let them know.

We lived in a second floor apartment. As I screamed and cried through another contraction, a car horn blared outside. I thought, *I know this man is not honking his horn outside for me to come down the stairs and just jump in the car!*

I crawled naked to the window. Below it waited my husband's gray 1987 Maximum. I could only look at him in disgust! This man was outside honking his horn for me to stroll out to his car!

With the little bit of strength that I had, I raised the window and yelled, "What the hell are you doing?"

He yelled, "Come downstairs!"

I yelled back at him, "I can't come downstairs! I need help!"

He finally trotted upstairs, saw me crawling on the floor naked, helped me get dressed, and drove me to the hospital.

Eighteen hours later I had a beautiful nine-pound-two-ounce baby girl, Janay. She became my reason for being.

I now knew what true love was.

Over the next months, Bob continued to receive phone calls and beeper pages from his past girlfriends and women coworkers. I told Bob he had six months to get his act together, or I was leaving and taking my baby with me.

In August 1990, Bob hadn't gotten it together. I left and took my baby to my mother's house.

(While there, I learned that Sonya, who had grinded on my leg in the coat closet in first grade, had been molested by members of her family when she was very little.)

For more than a year, Bob kept trying to get back together, but each time ended in another breakup.

In early 1992 we moved to a two-bedroom apartment in Passaic Park, New Jersey. Our relationship noticeably improved. We even did a TV segment for CNBC on young families making it in New Jersey. I interned at CNBC at the time while also finishing school.

That year I graduated from Montclair State University with my bachelor's degree in communication studies. Then I was hired as an assistant to the director at CNBC! Yay!

Soon after, Bob and I separated again.

Bob still worked in New York. Although he told me he slept in a room at his mother's house, I later found out that was a lie.

We both began to date other people.

Then Bob and I decided to start all over and make our marriage work. On July 4, 1992 we decided to try for a second baby. Four weeks later I was pregnant.

Unfortunately, I still had strong feelings that Bob was cheating on me.

One Wednesday, when I was about seven months pregnant, I didn't go to work because I had a prenatal appointment. Before I left for the doctor's, our telephone rang. A familiar female voice that I couldn't place asked for Bob. When I said, "He's not here," she hung up the phone.

I called the phone number back. As I did, it dawned on me that the familiar voice had been that of my elementary school best friend and maid of honor, Cassey.

On the other end, someone picked up the phone.

I said, "Cassey, is that you?"

"Yes."

I asked, "Why are you calling my house asking for my husband, Cassey?"

She had nerve to say, "You need to ask your husband about that!"

I cussed her out! I screamed at her and told her, "I am going to beat your ass, pregnant and all! In fact, I'm going to tell your mother and your father who you really are! I hate you!"

Her parents and I were very close; she used to be my best friend.

Cassey lived on the first floor of the two-family house that her parents owned. I drove over and rang the upstairs and downstairs doorbells, Cassey would not open the door. Her mother answered the door. I told her parents what had happened, crying now, devastated that my best friend had been messing around with my husband!

Back at home I called Bob. He had gall to cop an attitude and then lie to me.

I felt devastated. So there I was, seven months pregnant with a two-year-old baby, and finally my husband was truly showing me who he was.

We separated.

On April 9, 1993 I was so tired of being pregnant and wanting to give birth that my two-year-old, Janay, and I danced in my living room, and I marched as if I was still in my Eastside High School Marching 100 band playing the drums like I used to. I was so ready for this baby to come out!

The very next morning I went into labor. My daughter Evonne was born at 1:07 in the afternoon.

A couple of weeks went by. Bob came to visit and said, "I want to come home and get back together to work on our marriage."

I told him, "No, we can't get back together right now. There is so much hurt and pain, and I can't trust you."

For months we spoke occasionally about our relationship.

I was still close to his family and sometimes brought the children to Sunday dinners at his grandmother's house. Bob actually lived with his mother now, and we established a visitation schedule.

One day I drove the kids over to his mother's house so he could spend time with them. He wasn't there but his mother and another family member were. I stayed for a little while visiting.

While we talked, I noticed a photograph of Bob's mother holding a little boy. The boy appeared to be around the same age as our youngest daughter.

And he looked like Bob.

I asked Bob's mother, "Who's that cute little boy in the picture with you?"

She said, "He's Bob's godson."

"Godson? Who are his mother and father?"

"I don't know."

I said "okay," but in my mind and in my gut, something wasn't right. Bob's mother kept well informed and knew just about everything going on with her son.

When Bob's mother walked into another room out of earshot, the family member said, "That little boy is not Bob's godson. That's his son! They just don't want you to know."

"How old is he?"

"He's the same age as your baby daughter. And, Bob doesn't really live here either."

Soon after, someone else confirmed what Bob's family member had said.

Bob and I never lived under the same roof again.

For myself, I discovered that when a spouse cheats, it basically becomes a death of the original marriage and relationship. Then you have to mourn what you had before, because you'll never feel the same way about the spouse who committed adultery.

Although you may feel love for them, the trust is tarnished, and that's a difficult thing for many people to overcome.

Other people can overcome adultery in marriage, but the original marriage is dead and the new marriage will be different. Prayerfully, the relationship will be more mature, and both parties will have a better understanding of what it takes to have a successful marriage.

However, to enjoy the best and most enduring relationship possible, both spouses need to remember that marriage is sacred, and they need to keep it that way.

In 1992 I applied to, and was accepted into, the counseling graduate school at Montclair State University. I started work on my master's degree in guidance and family counseling.

As a single mother striving to take care of two beautiful daughters, I had to fight for child support because my husband only wanted to pay $50.00 per child per week. But I had hope, because I would graduate with a master's degree and find employment in the student affairs profession—prayerfully at a college or university far from New York and New Jersey. My girls and I needed a fresh start.

I was a very good resident assistant and was able to help my classmates and wondered if I could help people professionally. I had my own personal issues of dealing with or not dealing with issues of molestation and wanted to learn how to help myself become a better person, mom, daughter, sister, and friend.

I went to counseling for a couple of reasons number one I was going through divorce and my marriage was crap, and I knew my family was going to need counseling. My marriage was bad. I had two children, and now I will be a single mother and I needed to figure out the best way to raise my children. My main concerns were what am I going to do and how I am going to help these children? They had been through so much, and their father was not here. He was out there doing whatever he was doing, and I am their mother and I have my own issues. How am I going to be a good mother to my children? I was also the person in my family, and I still am that person who my family talks to just about anything and I'm a good listener. I wanted to be able to help my family, friends, and married couples.

Though it was a two-year counseling program, I was so focused on getting my degree that I finished the program in a year and a half.

I provided some marriage counseling while I was in my master's program. I know you are probably saying "marriage counseling? How can you give marital advice while going through a divorce?" My answer is simple. I like to help people! Family is important to me.

My first husband and I tried to keep it together. We were apart, together, apart, together, and somewhere in the midst of my marriage trials, I was counseling other couples—I still wanted to help other people stay married although I was going through hell.

God does not put us through anything just for the sake of us going through it. There is always a lesson in the blessing. You may not see it now, but hold on and everything will be revealed to you in time.

Reader, please take note. You may go through some similar situations, heartaches and pain. Please know that whatever you've been through, you can turn it around and use it for good. You can take that old baggage and use it for good to help people who may be going through the same or similar thing. You can help avoid people from making the same mistakes you made. Share what happened to you and prayerfully they will listen and learn versus going through the fire themselves. Misery does not have to have company!

Bob Barnes Jr. filed for divorce.

Derek's story

During the time that I was going through my divorce, when I was in graduate school, I was one of the directors of the gospel choir at school and church. One of the pianists named Derek and I met one day after rehearsal. He and I always talked about the choir and life in general. Derek was always jovial in the Lord. But this particular day he was not like his normal self. At that time, I was an older married woman now, so I'm not just a young girl in the choir.

After rehearsal, we went to get something to eat because he looked like there was something heavy on his mind.

I asked, "Are you okay?"

"Girl, you just don't know!"

"Do you need to talk?"

"Do you have time?"

"Yes, let's just go get something to eat." We went to a nearby diner. New Jersey's diners are open 24/7. "Are you all right?"

"I can't take it anymore!"

"You can't take what anymore?"

"I can't take my wife anymore I'm tired!"

"What are you talking about? Do you mean you're tired of your wife?"

"Yes!

She's a nice woman, and they had two children at the time.

"I just can't take it anymore. I am tired of her! She is messy! I'm working my full-time job and then at night, I am coming out here for the choir, and I play the piano for many different churches. I come home, and the house is a mess! I come home from work, and the house is not clean. I come home, and there is nothing to eat. I am just tired. I am working all the time. And I am tired of my wife!"

"Okay, wait a minute." While he was talking, I had put on my counseling hat and prayed and asked God to give me the right words to say to him.

"I want to get a divorce! I am sick of her!"

I just listened to him for a while and nodded my head to let him know that I was listening to him. Once he finished sharing how he felt, I began to ask him some questions about his marriage. I reiterated some of the things he said to make sure I understood what he was sharing with me.

"Let me share with you my philosophy on marriage (1) it is the easiest thing to do; (2) it's the hardest thing to maintain and (3) it is the hardest thing to get out of especially if you have children." He sat and thought about it for a while.

"What do you mean?"

"Marriage is the easiest thing you can do because anybody could just jump up and get married. But marriage is the hardest thing to maintain. Both people are attempting to take two individuals, and have them work together as one."

I displayed the example by utilizing my two pointer fingers and having them spread apart. As I was talking about bringing two people together to work as one, I brought my two hands closer together, with my pointer finger sticking up and put them together as one finger one in the back of the other.

"You aim to work together as one and that is a very difficult task sometimes, especially, if you don't have the Lord in your life. I know you have God in your life. You would not be sitting here talking about your marriage or ministering to people, and pouring God's word into so many people every week."

"But I can't take it anymore. I want a divorce!"

"Look, I heard everything that you said. I understand everything that you said about her. May I ask you a question?"

"Sure."

"If she were sitting here with me what would she say about you?" He sat and thought about it, and he was quiet for a couple of minutes. "I just want you to think about it. If she was sitting here with me what would she say about you? What complaints would she say about you?"

After naming about 5 to 8 different things that she would say about him. I explained "We all have complaints about the other spouse and we are quick to point the one finger at the other person.

We must remember that while we are pointing that one finger towards the other person we have three fingers pointing back at us. We must look in the mirror and check out what type of partner we are. Are we giving? Loving? Caring? Considerate? Showing concern? Being attentive, are we taking care of our responsibilities? Are we being honest with our partner? Are we trying or are we giving up? Are we praying together? Are we intimate?"

"Wow. I never thought about it like that."

"We should work to make sure we are meeting the needs of the other person as well as taking care of ourselves. We must work together as one and keep God first in our lives, and then the sky is the limit to what you can accomplish together."

"Now I feel bad. I am just very frustrated!"

"Please don't feel bad, it is okay to share your feelings. I knew something was wrong when I saw you. You just looked like you had a lot on your mind. Sitting here and talking about how you feel is a great start. Understanding that you need someone to talk is a good thing. That is half of the battle."

"Never thought we would need marriage counseling."

But please know that marriage can be the hardest thing to maintain if you have partners who are not willing to talk and take a closer look in the mirror. May I be transparent with you?"

"Sure"

"I am going through hell in my marriage right now. And I am trying to get out of my marriage. I could sit here and tell you all of the bad things that happened in my marriage and how we didn't work together and how we didn't overcome so many obstacles.

There were extramarital affairs, an additional child, and court battles over child support and property. We have so much going on. I am a testament to you that you don't want to go through what I'm going through right now. It's a living hell! You don't want to go through that. You don't want to go through that! Do you love your wife?

"Yes but."

"Yes but. I don't want to hear the 'buts'; I just want to know if you love your wife?"

"Yes I love her."

"Does she love you?"

"Yes she loves me."

"Well then you can make it work. Do you want to make it work?"

"Yes but…"

"Here you go again with the yes 'but.'"

"Do you want to make it work? If the answer is yes, then you will need to go to counseling. You both need to pray and ask God to help your marriage."

"Are you serious?"

"Yes! Just like I'm sitting here talking to you, you both need to go to counseling together and individually to talk about the issues you both are having. You need to find a counselor that you both feel comfortable talking to. If you're going to go to marriage counseling with someone from the church that is fine; however, I would also suggest that you find a professional marriage counselor too."

"Okay, I will think about it.

"Okay. Please know that I am coming to you from the heart because I know your wife, and I know you and you have a good heart. I met your three little kids. So at this point it's not just about you and your wife. Now it's about your three little people."

"Wow. I wasn't even thinking about how things would affect them."

"Do you want your children to grow up without a mommy and or a daddy at home? He sat quietly and was thinking about what I just said. In essence, it was significant to be able to pull on his heart strings and have him think more about how his actions may impact the lives of his three children.

As a result of our one session, he decided to work on his marriage instead of divorce; attend counseling and look a little closer at his actions versus pointing the finger at his wife.

As of this year, they have been married for 30 years. Their three children are beautiful adults and have families of their own; working in the ministry.

Derek is a musical genius and performs on television for very popular award shows and is a producer for several famous musicians and singers. It's amazing to see that they've been married over 30 years now, and to know that he was on the verge of getting a divorce.

I thank God for trusting me to counsel him toward his marriage versus toward divorce, although my life and marriage were a hot mess. God granted me wisdom, concern and the ability to be able to be used as a vessel to help his children save their marriage. Misery did not get any company that day.

God loves marriage and hates divorce because it breaks up the family unit and allows the enemy to come steal, kill, and destroy.

I moved from Passaic Park to Montclair, New Jersey, where I was blessed with a graduate assistantship as the Weekend Party Coordinator for the Student Activities Office at Montclair State University. Previously I had worked as a student leader. Now I was the staff person that student leaders had to work with in order to fundraise for their respective organizations.

It was a great opportunity for me to continue to work with students, but now on a professional level. This graduate assistantship paid for tuition, and I received a monthly stipend to help pay for my living expenses.

Dean James E. Harris, Chuck Feiner, Margaree Coleman Carter, Marsha Young, and Robin Hamlett-Dock were my saving graces. It was hard and I realized early that I needed to continue with my education. I could still hear Mr. Clark's voice in my mind saying, "Pinky, leave those boys alone and get your education!"

After the divorce, I changed my last name back to my maiden name.

My new life with my daughters began.

In March 1995 I was blessed with an opportunity to attend the ACPA Convention in Boston, Massachusetts. (ACPA is a registered trademark of the American College Personnel Association). During the convention, job applicants and employers participate in the largest and most comprehensive job placement service in student affairs.

I was able to interview with forty different colleges and universities in one weekend, and received job offers from several different institutions of higher learning. I found that Miami University in Oxford, Ohio, was a perfect fit for me and my children.

In July the girls and I moved to Ohio. A great benefit of working in student affairs and residence life was that I received as part of my compensation a beautiful fully furnished two-bedroom apartment, a full meal plan for me and my children, a housekeeping staff that cleaned my apartment once a week, a competitive salary, and my office was just outside my apartment.

I loved my job. I loved that God had enabled me to move away from all the negativity that I experienced during the divorce.

The professional staff members were phenomenal and very supportive. Among my colleagues, I made new lifelong friends. I was happy.

It didn't matter that I was the only African American female First Year Academic Advisor/ Hall Director.

Excerpt from my diary—Fast Forward—May 29, 1996

It's been a very long time since I even thought about writing down my most intimate thoughts!

I am a very happy person. God has blessed me abundantly. Let's see. Currently, I'm twenty-eight years old, divorced with two lovely, happy, little, sweet daughters. Of course, I got the best two things out of the not-so-good marriage. Janay and Evonne. I love them so much! My true loves!

Janay is six years old, and Evonne is three. We live in Oxford, Ohio, where I work as a hall director /first-year advisor at Miami University in Tappin Hall, a residence hall of 320 women whose wellbeing I am responsible for.

I am so blessed! God has brought me safely from a bad marriage, debt, loneliness, bitterness, and struggles, and He's brought us out of New Jersey and New York. I wanted to raise my children in a different environment. Miami University is a beautiful, slow-paced place where I can learn and continue to grow, and my children are allowed to be children and not have to deal with the negativity of my past.

I am blessed to be doing the job I've always wanted to do. I'm also the academic adviser for the women who live in my residence hall. I love my job!!! I love what I do!! And my girls are happy!

The divorce was finalized on July 11, 1995—THANK GOD!!! I received my master's degree right before the divorce. I'm so happy I didn't allow single motherhood and everything else stop me from achieving my goals. I love the Lord with all of my heart!

I believe God has a special plan for me, because I've had to deal with a lot of struggles, heartaches, and pains as well as success! I've been able to help people who may not have been able to handle certain situations without some assistance. I'm glad I was able to be there for them, and that God has been there for me as well.

Guess what? I legally changed my middle name to Pinky! Yay!!! It cost me $50.00—not bad!

In 1997 I attended the ACPA convention again and interviewed with several different colleges and universities. I had the pleasure of interviewing with the staff from the College of William & Mary in Williamsburg, Virginia, and was offered an opportunity to work with them. I accepted, and my daughters were welcomed with open arms.

Again I received as part of my compensation a beautiful, fully furnished two-bedroom apartment, a meal plan, and a competitive salary. My responsibilities definitely increased from being responsible for 320 students to well over 1000 students and several residence halls verse one.

I loved my job.

And, like Mr. Clark had inspired us to, I was standing on my own.

9 HEMA DEUX

The years drifted by, and I continued to yearn for the love of my father. Whenever I saw a commercial on television featuring a little girl and her father, or a movie with a little girl and her father, or any picture of a man and his little girl, those visuals tore me up inside.

I always wondered what my life would have been like if my father had been in it. Maybe he could have protected me from all the people who hurt me.

Even after that awful visit to Joplin, Missouri a decade earlier, I still wanted to get to know my father.

One day I contacted my mother and asked about my father again. She began to tell me more about his brothers, and I wanted to meet them.

She put me in contact with my Uncle Moose and Uncle Eddie.

When I called my Uncle Eddie, he welcomed me over the phone in a way that still makes me cry! He was so happy to hear my voice and wanted to meet me in person.

I went to visit him, and he hugged me very tightly as if I were his child! I cried like a baby while we hugged! He told me stories about him and my father growing up and shared some family photos with me.

He asked me if I wanted to meet his brother, my other uncle, who was known as Moose. Of course, I said yes! Uncle Eddie arranged a meeting.

Like Uncle Eddie, my Uncle Moose hugged me and welcomed me with open arms. His wife, Janice, also welcomed me into the family! We bonded very well, and they told me I could visit anytime.

I found myself visiting them often. They told me stories about my father and his wife, along with information about my four siblings, three of whom I didn't know I had. I actually have three older sisters and one older brother.

My sisters had graduate degrees and were successful.

One day when I visited, my Uncle Moose showed me a picture of his mother, my grandmother. I looked just like her, glasses and all. I was happy to see that I looked like someone in my father's family.

That day I smiled at the good, just as much as I cried over the bad. My grandmother had passed away.

I began to pray that God please not allow me to see or meet my father again when he lay in his casket, but to allow me to talk with my father, and to find out why he was never in my life.

I also asked God to inspire my father to tell me that he loved me, even if he only ever said it once.

As time went on, my uncles and Aunt Janice asked my father to meet with me again. He told them he would not be able to honor my request because of his wife. Apparently, she was adamant about my father not having a relationship with me.

Years passed, and I continued to have a visiting relationship with my uncles and aunt. I often visited them when I felt depressed about my father. They were able to help me feel better.

I began to realize that they loved me and wanted to help me. I will always be grateful to them for sharing my family history with me. However, the love and acceptance that I was yearning for had to come from my father. They were not able to fill his shoes.

In 1999 I met my soul mate, Daryl L. Miller, a handsome, dark-skinned man who was also an alum of my elementary school, Public School Number 24, and Eastside High School.

Come to find out, he actually had a crush on me while we were in high school.

We met (again) in May of 1999. Fifteen days later, he asked me to marry him.

I said, "Yes!" We were in our early thirties; we both knew what we wanted.

We both had children. I had two beautiful daughters, and he had one handsome son. Blended families can be difficult, but we were able to handle the challenges, and the blessings, that came with blending a family.

Within six months we married.

Yes, I know you're saying, "What? Six months? Didn't you learn your lesson from your previous marriage?"

And I say, yes I did. I also prayed fervently about my next husband, and God brought him to me. I was not seeking him. The day we re-acquainted, God told me he was my husband—I heard him speak in my heart—and I was obedient.

When you know, you know!

I was blessed again to have another job in student affairs. This time I became an assistant director, and later the interim director, of residence life at St. Peter's College in New Jersey. Perks were very similar to those of my previous positions, and included a fully furnished four-bedroom home with a basement.

In 2000, I was thirty-three years old and pregnant with my third daughter. I continued my relationship with my father's brothers, my uncles and my aunt.

One day while I was visiting my Aunt Janice, she showed me photographs of my sisters at a recent family event. As I looked at the pictures, I began to cry. I felt so unloved by my father and was deeply saddened that I had siblings who had families, and I was not part of their family.

My children have aunts and uncles they don't know. It was so unfair.

The pictures revealed my resemblance to my siblings, and their children and my children resembled each other as well.

Described in two words: It hurt. It was a blessing, but it hurt!

My Aunt Janice hugged me and told me that everything was going to be okay.

Then she said my father was coming to Paterson the following weekend for an Elks banquet, and maybe I could meet him, because his wife was not coming with him.

We devised a plan that I would call her while he was there, then she would hand him the phone.

That weekend came. Aunt Janice called me and told me to call back in five minutes.

I was elated at the thought of finally being able to speak with my father!

I waited four minutes, then called her house.

She answered the phone and said to my father, "The phone is for you."

He asked, "Who is it?"

She didn't say, but handed him the phone.

I thought my heart would beat right out of my chest. The anticipation was so great, I could hardly contain myself.

He said, "Hello?"

I said, "Hello!" You know me by now. I began to sob.

He said, "Who this is?"

"Olandha, your daughter."

There was a pause.

He said, "How are you doing?"

I said, "Fine" as I cried.

"Why are you crying?"

"Because I want to get to know you."

"It's okay. Don't cry."

He asked me about my recent second marriage, and who my new husband was, and if he was a good guy. He then asked about my pregnancy. "So this makes baby number three for you, right?"

"Yes." I was flabbergasted that my father, whom I've wanted to get to know all of my life, knew these intimate details about me before I even shared them with him.

He asked questions about me obtaining my master's degree. We were actually having a conversation, as if we talked on a regular basis. He asked questions a caring father would ask.

We talked for about fifteen minutes. I gave him my phone number, and he agreed to call me.

Unfortunately, he never did.

More years went by, and I continued to yearn to be close to my father.

One day I researched my father's whereabouts in Joplin, Missouri found a phone number, and called the number.

A young woman's voice answered the phone. I asked to speak to Olin.

She asked, "Whose calling?"

I said, "This is Olandha."

Through the phone I heard tension going on in the background. I asked her, "Who is this?"

She said her name, and I realized this was one of my sisters. I believed this was my oldest sister whose hair Leah (my cousin) had once braided.

Someone on her end said, "Why is she calling here? Why is she calling here?"

My father got on the phone. "Who this is?"

I said, "This is Olandha."

He said, "Don't call here anymore!" Then I heard a dial tone.

I must have called at the wrong time.

In 2001 I was blessed to be pregnant again with another daughter, and I was blessed with another job as the director of residence life at Clark Atlanta University, a historically black college.

As before, the job came with perks. I had a four-bedroom apartment on campus, and my family and I lived there for a few months while we had our house built.

Working at a historically black college provides the opportunity to share your talents with students who may share your culture. Singing the alma mater is one strategy that is very significant for instilling pride within students and the school. I had the pleasure of working at two historically black colleges and singing the alma mater was very sacred. All students had to learn and sing the alma mater at prominent assemblies and other events very much like my experiences at Eastside High School.

I loved my job dearly. It came with a competitive salary, and I was living in Atlanta, Georgia!

A few years went by. I attended graduate school and worked on my Ph.D., plus I took care of my family of five children along with my new husband.

I have a very strong relationship with God, and he places things in my heart and in my spirit that I cannot explain. He often nudges me awake at four or five in the morning, and awakens my spirit to do something! To move on something!

And I have to move! One very significant lesson I had to learn was to listen and do what God tells you to do, *when* he says, "Do it!"

Around my birthday in March 2009, God began to nudge my spirit about my father. I felt him telling me, "Something isn't right."

Since I was busy, I brushed it off. But that feeling kept coming back to me over and over again!

I shared with my husband that something wasn't right with my father; I said I didn't know what it was, but something was wrong!

With me in graduate school full-time, I didn't have a full-time job, and our financial situation was strained. We had a five-bedroom home and a family of seven, with children in college, high school, and private elementary school.

Finally I realized that I had to move and do what God said to do.

I knew that I could no longer call my father, and that whatever was going on was serious enough for me to travel to Joplin, Missouri.

Because I hadn't kept in close contact with my uncles and Aunt Janice in recent years, I attempted to find an address for my father with limited knowledge. An Internet search produced ten different Olin Bronson's, and none of them had phone numbers that matched the telephone number I had for him.

I had ten possibilities but was totally unsure.

The next problem was that I had no money to travel. God led me to my Delta Airline Sky Miles that I had never used. I found out they were due to expire within the next couple of weeks.

When I contacted the airline, the representative told me I had just enough Sky Miles to cover the round-trip flight to Joplin, Missouri.

Alone, I flew to Joplin on a Friday, rented a car, and drove address to address without a GPS system, starting with the one closest to the airport. I'd brought printed copies of MapQuest directions, and of course I got lost.

I started losing it because I didn't know where I was going, and it was beginning to get late.

One of the addresses led me to the same beautiful house I'd gone to when I'd traveled to Missouri the first time, at nineteen years old. Seeing the house brought back hurtful memories. I remembered my father just sitting on the staircase, staring at me.

For a time I sat in the car and admired this gorgeous new home, wondering what it would've been like to live in this beautiful home with my father, or at least to visit with my four siblings that I never had the pleasure of meeting.

I prayed to God that this encounter, in which I would meet my father for the third time, would be much different from our second encounter back in 1987.

But just in case I had to do an expedited exit, I took some pictures of the home.

My nerves surfaced and began to rattle me. After gathering my courage, I walked up to the house and rang the doorbell.

Long moments passed. Then a woman answered the door.

She said, "Hello. May I help you?"

"Hello, I'm Olandha. Do you remember me?"

"Yes, I know who you are." To my surprise, she said, "Come in."

Thank you so much, God!

She welcomed me in the house and closed the door. As I stood in the foyer, she asked, "Why you are here?"

"I had a gut feeling that something was wrong with my father. I just had to come and find out if he is all right."

She took a deep breath. "He is suffering from colon cancer."

I gasped. "Did the doctors give him a timeline to live?"

"About six months."

"Can I see him?"

"Yes, he's downstairs. You can go downstairs."

"Thank you!" I started downstairs, then stopped in my tracks and turned to her. "I need to apologize to you."

She asked, "Why do you need to apologize to me?"

"I need to apologize to you for my existence, and for the hurt that my being here has caused you." I began to cry. "I know my being here has hurt you and your marriage. I experienced a similar situation in my first marriage. My older daughters have a brother who was not conceived by me, so I truly know how you feel."

She gave me a hug. Then I went downstairs to visit with my father.

The finished basement had been beautifully decorated. I stopped on the bottom step, looked around, and noticed that on a large sectional couch in front of me, which faced a big flat-screen television, a short, dark-skinned man sat, thin and covered with a blanket.

As I walked toward him, he turned around and looked at my face.

I said, "Hello."

"Hello."

I asked him, "Do you know who I am?"

"No."

"I'm your daughter Olandha."

He said, "Hi. How are you?"

"Could I sit down?"

He nodded.

I sat close to him, and told him about my journey to finding him. "I knew something wasn't right, and God led me to find you." He listened as I shared with him that I was working on my PhD, and showed him pictures of his grandchildren. He was very pleased to see the pictures.

He asked, "How is your mother?"

"She's fine." I had so much that I wanted to know. "Would it be okay if I asked you some questions?"

"Sure."

"Why were you not in my life?"

He pointed toward the stairs. "It was because of her." His wife.

"Why did you decide not to have anything to do with me even though you know I existed?"

"You just don't understand. She made me make a choice. She told me, 'You can either have your family, or you can have that child, but you cannot have both of us!'" So he had to make a decision. "I chose my wife and four children."

142

What could I say? In a way I understood, and in another way, I didn't. Because in my mind if you're mature enough to have sex, then a man and/or woman should be mature enough to take care of the responsibilities that come with having unprotected sex.

He could have given my mother some money, or sent money through the mail, or via his brothers or other friends who knew my mother. He could have called from time to time. He could have written letters. He could have visited now and then.

The time was getting late. I said, "I plan to be here for the weekend. Will you allow me to come back tomorrow and see you again?"

"Yes. Yes, come back tomorrow, so that you can meet your sister."

My eyes began to tear up. *Meet my sister?!*

I was so excited and thankful to God! Not only had I been welcomed into the house, I also officially met my father—after an entire lifetime, he'd finally acknowledged me! And now I could meet my sister!

Before I said goodbye to my father, I went upstairs to ask his wife permission to come back the next day. She said yes, but asked that I give her my number and she would call me, because my father had a doctor's appointment on Saturday.

I said, "No problem. Thank you, I truly appreciate you," and gave her my phone number.

Then I went back downstairs to say goodbye to my father.

He asked, "Are you going to come back tomorrow?"

"Yes, but I have to wait for your wife to call me because she said you have a doctor's appointment tomorrow."

His expression turned to stone. "I don't have a doctor's appointment tomorrow!"

I said, "Okay, well, I'll be back tomorrow; I just have to wait until she calls me."

I gave my father—*my father!*—a hug and a kiss on the cheek. He hugged me back.

In my rental car, I cried my eyes out and thanked God for the opportunity, and that he softened my father's wife's heart to allow me to visit with my father.

The next day, I woke up early in my hotel room and began the hours-long wait for the phone to ring.

His wife didn't call.

Two in the afternoon came and went.

I telephoned their house. No one answered.

I drove back to their house.

A young woman answered the door. "Hello." She had a very soft voice. "May I help you?"

I couldn't help staring. I was looking at a young woman who looked very much like me. We both had very short hair, we both wore glasses, and our features resembled each other's very closely, except that my skin color was a little lighter than hers.

I asked, "Are you one of the sisters?"

"Sisters?"

"One of the sisters—Olin's daughter."

"Yes."

My sister! I exclaimed, "I'm a sister too!"

"What?"

Excited, I said, "I'm Olin's daughter too!"

She looked at me in astonishment, and I looked at her in astonishment, then she invited me into the house.

As we stood there looking at each other in amazement, she said, "I can't believe what you're saying! I have another sister!"

And I said, "I can't believe I'm meeting one of my sisters!"

We hugged each other and cried! *I was hugging my sister!* As she stood there stunned that I existed, I shared the story of how I came to visit when I was nineteen years old, and described what the house looked like then.

As I described details, she stood listening with her mouth opened. She said, "I can't believe it!"

I told her about the verbal exchange with her mother, then I shared with her that I'd contacted our brother, Olin Jr, just a few years ago, and that he was stunned as well. He'd told me that he wanted to talk with his parents about it and that he would call me back. However, I had not heard back from him.

She said, "Wow! This all makes sense now. Maybe that's why my brother stayed away from the family for a while a few years back."

I asked, "Is your mother here?"

"No, she isn't."

"Is father here? Your mother told me yesterday that he had a doctor's appointment today."

"He didn't have a doctor's appointment today. He's downstairs. You can go visit with him."

Downstairs, I was very happy to see him again, but also frustrated with the fact that they hadn't told my sister that I had been there just yesterday. They should have prepared her for our meeting.

After my father and I talked for a few minutes, I said, "I'm concerned that you didn't tell my sister about me. She was almost in shock."

He said, "You just don't understand!"

A while later I went upstairs to find my sister because I wanted to exchange contact information with her. I called to her and finally found her in the garage. When she came into the house, I could clearly see that she was very upset, and must have been crying for several minutes.

I asked, "Are you okay?"

She continued to cry. "They didn't tell me anything! I don't know why they didn't tell me about you!"

"I'm sorry that they didn't tell you! I am so sorry!"

We hugged each other, and looked at each other, and said, "I have a sister!" and we hugged each other again. We talked about ages and our birthdays. I was the baby sister, by just one year. We exchanged information and promised to call each other.

Back downstairs, I spent more time with my father. As we talked, I needed to bring some closure to the many questions that I had.

My father said, "I am sorry! I am sorry for not being in your life!"

I loved hearing that. I loved hearing it so much that I couldn't help crying. My father gave me a hug. I soaked in every heartbeat of it.

As we continued talking, I began to get an uneasy feeling, as if an uneasy spirit permeated the basement. I distinctly heard God say to me, "It's time to go. It's time to go."

I prepared to leave, but such goodbyes aren't instantaneous. Nearly half an hour passed.

Suddenly, I heard movement upstairs. Then someone briskly descended the stairs.

His wife appeared angry that I was in her home. "You need to leave!"

I gathered the rest of my things.

"You can visit him," she said, "but you cannot visit him here!" Then she went upstairs and waited for me to leave.

As I picked up my belongings, I left my business cards between the sections of the couch, and I left my business cards with my father.

I hugged him and said goodbye.

He said, "I am very proud of you! And I love you!" He kissed my cheek and I kissed his back.

I said, "I love you too!" I squeezed him tightly, then headed upstairs.

He was proud of me, and he loved me. My father had said he loved me. In that moment, my heart was full.

At the top of the stairs, his wife glared at me. "Do *not* to come back to my home!"

My sister stood near her, crying. What was going on?

I thanked my father's wife then left.

On my way back to the hotel, I sobbed. It was a miracle I didn't cause an accident. Yesterday his wife had invited me in. Why was she acting today like she had when I visited back when I was nineteen?

After I'd returned back home, I realized I'd misplaced my sister's contact information. I didn't find it anywhere. Even phone calls to the hotel and car rental agency didn't produce it. I was devastated. She didn't live with her parents; she lived in another part of town, and I might have been able to have a relationship with her.

I tried to find her on the Internet but was unsuccessful.

As the months went by, I continued to feel very sad at finding her, only to lose her again. Yet I was also grateful to God that I'd met her and got to know her and my father a little. Grateful that my father answered a lifetime of questions. Grateful to hear him tell me he loved me. Grateful to hear he was proud, and that he was sorry for not being in my life.

During that brief visit, God had given me the desires of my heart. I belonged to both of my families. One much more than the other, but I belonged.

In September 2009, my mother telephoned me to tell me my father had passed away.

Though I knew his passing was inevitable due to the cancer, I was very saddened by the news.

When I asked for the funeral information, she said, "They already had the funeral. He passed away three months ago."

I felt devastated, because my father had passed away, and because his family didn't allow me to attend the funeral or to tell him goodbye. I would have appreciated even a private viewing.

An online search for his obituary turned up a family page where many, many friends and family members had left condolences. I read several. People had written awesome things about my father.

And I hadn't been permitted to know him.

In my anger and sadness, I wrote a message on his obituary page and let it be known that I was the fourth daughter of Mr. Olin Sr. I told the secret that had been hidden for forty-one years. In addition, I left my contact information. Undoubtedly this hurt his wife and my siblings, and for that I apologize. I had been denied and rejected due to nothing I had done, and punished a lifetime for the poor choice two people had made one evening four decades ago. I just wanted to be acknowledged by my father, and to have a relationship with my sisters and brother.

I pray to God that one day I'll get a phone call from at least one of my sisters or my brother, and hopefully they'll wish to have a relationship with me. I know it would be difficult for them, because they are loyal to their mother, and she has also been punished forty years for nothing she had done, and may continue to feel punished, simply because I exist.

In February 2010, I visited my father's grave in Missouri, I told him that I forgave him.

Forgiveness, I've learned, is critical in order to feel joy in life. You must forgive in order to get unstuck and move forward. That said, once you forgive people, it's okay to protect yourself from their hurting you again. Not everyone deserves a front seat in your life, and it is okay to love people and pray for them from a distance.

Forgiveness is key to a better and more fulfilling life.

I learned that from my mother.

I'd like to share another thought with you here. God does not make mistakes. God made you who you are. For a long time I described myself as a "mistake," and "accident." When asked, I said, "I'm the result of an adulterous affair." That's how I viewed myself. Frequently I thought that there must be something wrong with me, because my father did not want me.

I came to the realization that because my father was not involved in my life, I became who I am today. "Are not two sparrows sold for a penny? Yet not one of them will fall to the ground apart from the will of your Father" (Matthew 10:29 *NIV*). God allows each of us to experience what we do in order to help us fulfil our unique purposes in life. We experience nothing for ourselves alone. We experience it to make a positive difference for someone else.

I always wanted to be the best that I could be, so that if and when my father would accept me, he would be proud of me. In being my best, I can be of benefit to those whose lives I touch.

Although I never had the pleasure of calling my father daddy, my dad did tell me he was proud of me, and that was a prayer answered.

I love you, dad!

I am hema deux. A child of two bloods. Two families. My heart beats with the blood of both, and with great love for both.

10 Lean on Me

Amoli's Story

I was a night owl and was available to students when they needed me. One late evening I was walking around the residence halls when I noticed a student sitting on the couch in the lounge. I walked towards her to say hello. She appeared to be sad.

She was laying on the couch in the fetal position. Her cheeks were swollen, her face was red, and there were tears streaming down her face. She was trying to wipe them away as I approached her. But Mama Pinky could see through those things.

I said hello and asked her if it would be okay if I sat down. She said yes. She was a student that I saw in one of my buildings on a regular basis, but I did not know her name. I did not know names like Mr. Clark, but I recognized her. I sat on the edge of the sofa beside her but not too close.

"How are you doing? Can I help you with anything?"

"No."

"Why are you crying?" She did not answer.

I asked her softly, "Are you okay? It's late at night, why are you crying?" Tears were still streaming down her face.

"Is it okay if I sit a little closer?" She nodded her head yes as she wiped away her tears.

"I am Pinky. What is your name?"

"My name is Amoli." Amoli means precious in Hindi.

I sat quietly for a little while because I did not want to bombard her with questions.

"Is there anything that I can do?"

"No."

"It's late. I cannot leave you in the lounge by yourself. Maybe I can help. Did you go out tonight?"

"I went to a party."

"Were you with friends?"

"Yes."

"What party did you go to?"

"A fraternity party."

"Did something happen at the party?"

She was hesitant, "Well, well, well not really."

"What do you mean by not really?"

"Well no, not really."

"Okay." From my counseling training, I had a strong feeling that the words "not really" meant something happened. She was just not ready to share what happened to her at that specific moment.

Thursday nights were the party nights on this particular campus, as on most campuses. When she mentioned the word fraternity, I knew from experience that most likely the incident included alcohol or something sexually related.

"Did someone hurt you?"

"One of the guys kept touching me," she said softly

"What fraternity party did you go to?"

"Gamma Fraternity."

"Did anything else happen at the fraternity party?" She did not answer. I knew that I was on the right track and something else had happened because more tears began streaming down her face. She was not ready to share.

I patiently sat and waited. As the tears lessened, I began to ask more closed ended questions so that she could at least say yes or no. I hoped to gain more information because she was not talking much.

"Please know that whatever you say to me will stay with me, and that it is in confidence. But you do need to know if someone hurt you, we may have to seek additional help to make sure that you are okay."

"Did somebody hit you?"

"No."

"Did someone say something to you?"

"No." She started to talk a little more once she was able to recognize that I was trying to help her, not hurt her.

"Please tell me what happened at the party."

"I was dancing, and this guy came up very close to me from behind and I didn't like it. He kept touching me. I was telling him no! And was pushing him back with my hands, but he just kept coming closer and closer."

"Did you say stop?"

"Yes, I said stop. I left to go sit down and he followed me. He wouldn't leave until I moved closer to my girlfriends, then he backed off."

"Do you know him?"

"No."

"Had you seen him before?"

"Yes."

"Was this your first interaction with him?" The tears began to fall again. I slowed down my questions and patiently waited for her to respond.

"No, I saw him at another party before and we were in a bedroom." She began to cry harder and I hugged her. "He put his hand down my pants and would not let me go out of the room!" She sobbed. "I told him no! No! No! But he did it anyway!"

"I am so sorry! I am so sorry that happened to you. When did this happen?" I moved her hair out of her face.

"Last week."

"Oh my God! I am so sorry."

"Did you go the doctor or to the hospital?"

"No."

"Do you want to go the doctor or to the hospital?"

"No, no one can find out about this!"

"Okay." I waited until she calmed down.

"Is it okay if I ask you more questions?"

"Yes it's okay."

"Did you say no or stop?"

"Yes."

"Did you yell or scream?"

"No."

"Did he do anything else?"

"He tried to kiss me."

"Did you want him to kiss you?"

"No!"

"Did anything else happen?"

"No."

"How did you get out of the room?"

"I just got up off the bed, and I ran out of the room."

"Do you know him?"

"No, but I know what he looks like."

"Did anything else happen?"

"Do you mind if I share this information with my supervisor?"

Frantically she said, "I don't want anybody to know about this!"

"Okay, I understand. Well you know, it's getting late. Do you plan on staying down here in the lounge?"

"I want to stay down here for a little while longer."

"Would it be okay if I stayed here with you?"

"Yes, it's okay."

The conversation then moved away from what was going on. I did not want her to feel like I was badgering her. At that point I wanted to build a relationship with her and let her know that I was there for her.

"My office is over there, and I'm always here if you need me. You can knock on my door at any time. It doesn't matter what time it is, day or night." It was getting late and she wanted to go upstairs. "Would it be okay if I followed up with you tomorrow? Or can you come to my office? I just want to make sure you are okay."

"Yes that is fine."

"Okay, goodnight."

She went into her room, and I went back to my office. I wrote up an incident report so that I could review it in the morning. The next day I went to my supervisors and let them know what was going on. I followed up with the student because she did not want anyone to know about the incident.

I created a rapport with her and she shared some things with me. She found out that there were a few other girls that this was happening to. She told me about the dowry.

"He knows that we won't tell because we would risk losing too much. We would dishonor our family and they would be ashamed."

Another week had gone by and Amoli and I seemed to talk more frequently. I continued to provide a status report to my supervisors, and during that time our student affairs staff was able to pinpoint the alleged perpetrator and kept an eye on him.

My office was in the lobby where a lot of students congregated. I was very active with my students. When I saw Amoli with a group of her friends, I would go over and ask how they were doing. I would ask about their classes and assist if necessary.

It was just a matter of being available and letting them know that I was someone they could trust. If they said something to me it would stay with me, sort of. As an administrator of the college, I could not keep these types of incidents confidential.

I shared all information with my supervisors to keep them aware of the situation, so that if and when the students were ready to share, they could. If they wanted to file a report or press charges, we would be able to do so.

As our relationship continued to build, I was able to ask her about her friends.

"Amoli, do you know if this happened to any of your friends?"

"Yes."

"Do you think they would like to talk about it?"

"I don't know."

"Do you think they would have a problem with me?"

"I don't know."

"Can you please check with them to see if they would feel comfortable talking to me?"

"Okay."

This relationship was very significant because I built a rapport with one student. She was then able to say to her friends, "Pinky is cool, she will help us."

As a result, her friends shared some intimate details of what happened to them. We were able to hold the male student accountable for his actions.

The university took swift action. The young man was expelled from the university and had to deal with legal issues. The women's offenses were kept private. It was their responsibility to do what they needed to do as far as sharing that information with their family and whoever they would marry.

We provided counseling to the students. We wanted to make sure that the students were physically, mentally, and emotionally healthy.

I was mad! I was angry at this young man for taking advantage of these young women. They were disrespected and abused. It was hurtful because I began thinking back to being manipulated and held hostage in a sense when I was being molested.

I felt very good about helping them. It was awesome to observe them blossom as first-year students and create new friendships. This is why it is so important for women to travel together and follow the buddy system when they live on college campuses.

Towards the end of the semester, Amoli's personality was different. She was not as withdrawn as she was when I first met her sitting on the couch.

Sometimes during the day, I would offer a kickboxing exercise program for all students. We watched the videos and did the exercises together in the lobby. Amoli would come to the program and do the kickboxing with me. We were working out together and having fun. She was a different student. She was more confident, she was more outgoing, and she was smiling more.

Sometimes when freshman students come to campus, it is their first time away from home. Some students have been sheltered by their families and may not know how to handle the freedoms and independence of residing on a college campus. They may not be as familiar with their new surroundings.

It was a learning experience and, unfortunately, that was one of the worst experiences anyone could have. I am glad that we were able to help all students involved. Thank God!

Moving Forward

In 2010, I was blessed with another job within student affairs, as an assistant dean of students at the University of South Dakota. Yes, I said South Dakota! Yes, it was cold, but as always I loved this job and the people. It was an experience I will never forget.

(Photo Joe Clark, sent to Dr. Pinky Miller upon completion of my doctoral studies- "Pinky, Never wait for your ship to come in, row out and meet it" Joe Clark – Lean On Me)

In 2011, I received my Doctor of Philosophy degree in educational policy studies - higher education from Georgia State University. I want to thank my dissertation committee for all of the challenges, support and love that I received. Dr. Gwen Benson, Dr. Karen Card (The University of South Dakota), Dr. Joyce King Dr. Lisa Martin-Hansen and Dr. Hayward Richardson.

In 2012, I became vice president of student affairs at Allen University in Columbia, South Carolina, another historically black college. A vast majority of historically black colleges and universities have major financial, budgetary strains, and as a result of low enrollment, I was released from the position, heartbroken. But I'm a survivor.

Passing the bullhorn

I believe that Mr. Clark has now passed the bullhorn over to his students so that we are now the ones that other people can lean on.

This book would not be complete, and my celebration of Mr. Clark's legacy would be insufficient, if I did not spotlight the great blessing that many teachers are to their students, even if students don't fully understand or express that during their years in the classroom.

Teachers have a great responsibility to their students, especially in the inner city. Students needs from one subculture to the next differ. Students not in the inner city or who live in rural areas have privileges that other students do not. For example, many rural students may be concerned about what homework assignment is due tomorrow. Many inner city students are trying to figure out what they are going to have for dinner tonight and breakfast tomorrow. Some inner city students come to school hungry because they didn't eat the night before. So they aren't necessarily worried about an assignment. They are concerned about survival.

Many inner city children go home or to another place that may be filled with drug addicts, alcoholics, domestic abuse, and/or molestation.

Teachers (and coaches, and administrators) are life changers— good, bad, or indifferent. Teachers have to make the tough decision as to what type of life changer they are going to be.

Teachers will make a lasting impact on their students' lives. Students will remember those teachers who took the time out to give them a hug, or encouragement, or to simply listen and care. Students will also remember those teachers who do not show any concern for their personal well-being.

Students can tell when a teacher is "faking the funk," "perpetrating a fraud," being fake, and trying to act like they care. Students can see right through fake teachers. Teachers need to be real! They need to show compassion for their students as human beings.

Teachers, I know students will get on your very last nerves. However, you as the teacher may need to have a broader scope, a broader lens with which to view, and a stronger heart with which to reach and teach that child who is an obnoxious, disrespectful, troublemaker. Few children are born angry and looking for a fight; they simply want to be loved, and react when that core, essential human need is terribly unfulfilled. You never know what might be going on with that child's home life.

Teachers need to be confidants for students, someone who a student can rely on and know that if he or she is in need of help, that teacher can and will help them.

Being a teacher, a principal, a coach, or an administrator is a major responsibility that should never be taken lightly. I know— that's far easier said than done, however, persistence overcomes resistance—Mr. Clark taught me that. Teachers must hold their students accountable for their actions, and sometimes they have to show tough love to their students, and at the same time find a good balance that can help students thrive in positive ways.

Teaching is one of the most significant careers in the world. Other than parenting, one would be hard pressed to find a career that made a greater difference to every young person's present and future.

Being able to share knowledge with others is truly great. Kids grow into adults who need knowledge in order to succeed and thrive. But equally as precious is giving kids positive attention, a caring shoulder, a listening ear, and an example of the human decency that is possible, which they might never encounter elsewhere.

Teachers and administrators *must* plant positive, caring seeds within their students, and then prayerfully those seeds will help students grow into positive, caring, hard-working, productive citizens of the world.

I had the awesome opportunity of having some phenomenal teachers and administrators who invested in me and my well-being. I'm still in contact with several of my elementary and high school teachers, including Mr. Clark, and they continue to let me know that they are proud of me. Even though I'm an adult with my own family, I still look up to them as my teachers, because they taught me so much—more than what was printed in textbooks—and they made themselves available to me.

Because I could lean on them, others can now *lean on me*.

***

A special word about Dr. Joe Louis Clark, whom we students at Eastside called "Mr. Clark."

Mr. Clark inspired me to be who I am today.

Mr. Clark told me, "Pinky, never wait for your ship to come in! Row out and meet it!" He also said, "*Pinky!* The big problem is you have to be focused! You got a find your raison d'être—your reason for being! When you find your reason for being, then our Creator has already equipped us with the mechanisms to endure all the hostilities that you're going to encounter."

For me and for thousands of students at Eastside, every one of whom he knew by name, Mr. Clark was the father we never had at home. He was someone I truly respected and asked for guidance and confided in if I ever had a problem.

He taught us teenage girls that we did not have to lower our standards for boys. He taught us all that education was vital, that God is significant, and that self-discipline can make all the difference.

He taught us that if we wanted something, we could go after it, and no one could stop us.

Mr. Clark also made us realize that our journey through high school was there to shape us into the adults we would ultimately become.

I'm not sure where I would be right now if it were not for him and my mom.

Thank you, Mr. Clark! I appreciate you for your time, your effort, your tenacity, your big words, your love, your respect that taught us to respect ourselves, your sacrifice, and most of all your heart. I thank you with the accomplishments of my life. I pray that you will know that your life's work was not in vain—you did a hell of good job.

I love you.

Know that whenever I encountered a challenge that appeared too tough for me to handle, I heard your loud voice in my ear telling me, "*Pinky!* You can do it!" I believed you just as you believed in me. I trust I can speak for the majority of my classmates:

Mr. Clark, you saved us.

APPENDIX

In August 2011, after completing my dissertation, I spoke with Mr. Clark in regard to turning my original research into a book and produce a Lean on Me Too movie. When I sent him my dissertation, he was flabbergasted.

He was so happy that he sent me an autographed poster of himself from the cover of Time Magazine and a basket of the edible fruit. He was elated. I believe I am the first student to receive her Ph.D. from his graduating class. He was very proud of me.

Mr. Clark introduced me to Norman Twain, the producer of *Lean on Me*, after reading my dissertation; he was very excited about the possibility. He shared my research with some of his colleagues and was informed that they did not believe there was a large enough audience interested in this endeavor.

Mr. Twain suggested that I produce a documentary instead to garner interest in the movie. Norman Twain introduced me to a producer, Randy Simon. We began filming and interviewing alumni and administrators for the documentary at EHS during our C'86, 25th Reunion and tour in November 2011. We are in the developing and fundraising stages to produce the Know Our Story documentary.

Where is Dr. Clark Now?

(Photo Courtesy of Senior Times magazine)

Dr. Clark continues to keep a sharp eye on America's schools that he still finds not much improved. In 2008, Dr. Clark received an honorary doctorate from the US Sports Academy. In 2012, Mr. Clark was on the cover of a Senior Times magazine. Mr. Clark is wearing a cowboy hat, a leather vest, over a white short sleeved shirt with a gold chain and gold horse medallion, holding a Louisville Slugger baseball bat resembling the 1988 picture of him on the cover of *Time Magazine*, displaying his ever-present bat and a sophisticated suit.

The headline: "Is getting tough the answer? School Principal Joe Clark says "yes' and the critics are up in arms"

(Photo Courtesy of *Senior Times* magazine Photo by TJ Morrissey / Lotus Studios)

According to Senior Times magazine, Dr. Clark stated that he loved the media when they were writing about him, and he was profiled in over 260 media reports (Amburn, 2012).Clark is in his mid-70s now and currently resides in Gainesville, Florida and has 10 acre horse farm in Newberry, Florida.

He's lived there for more than 15 years, and he has a beautiful landscape outside in front of the farm house that is surrounded by orange and blue rocks and other orange and blue novelties to resemble the Eastside High School colors. He stated that he is addicted to horses and he used to ride them for miles and he used to grow vegetables in his garden. He is retired and shared that his wife Gloria has been a very supportive wife, "without her I would have never been able to endure the pain inflicted on me by adversarial forces. She is a very good person and I have been blessed" (Amburn, 2012).

(Mr. Clark & wife Gloria, 2012 - Courtesy of Senior Times Photo by TJ Morrissey / Lotus Studios)

Lean on Me 25th Anniversary – 2014

February 2014 was the 25th Anniversary of the Lean on Me movie and the alumni are very excited to celebrate our history. In October 2013, the following logo was created by alum Keith Williams Class of 1984 to assist our efforts to raise funds and support the college education for the current students at Eastside High School. We understand the significance of furthering ones education and want to give back to those who may be less fortunate.

(Logo created by alum Keith Williams C'84)

I wish Warner Bros. would have considered creating some educational college scholarship fund as a consistent way of being able to give back to the inner city, poverty-stricken children who helped them generate millions of dollars back in 1989.

I am in hopes that Warner Bros. would join our annual efforts to give back to the students at Eastside High School. I created a tax deductible college scholarship fund for the current students at Eastside High School who are accepted into and enrolled in college. Please help me give back by making a taxable donation toward the $10,000.00 annual scholarships by going to my website Know-Our Story.com

Molestation

Molestation is defined as the crime of sexual acts with children up to the age of eighteen, including touching of private parts, exposure of genitalia, . . . inducement of sexual acts with the molester or with other children, variations of these acts by pedophiles, and any unwanted sexual acts with adults short of rape (*The Free Dictionary*, Copyright © 2013).

If someone is touching you in wrong places, showing you their body parts, or hurting you in any way, **you must tell someone who can and will help you, and keep telling people until someone helps you!**

The person behaving inappropriately toward you may be a family member, friend, neighbor, counselor, teacher, coach, pastor, or anyone else you know, and it may be a stranger.

Educators, if you have quiet kids, you have to watch them and look for signs of changes in their behavior. Young children do not know how to verbalize bad touches, but bad touches should be discussed twice per school year, every year. Wouldn't that have been amazing if I knew what that was and how to verbalize what was happening to me to my teacher? And the teacher could intervene and do something about it and find out what was going on in my family life.

Parents, please make sure that you watch and protect your children. Be very selective and careful who you will allow in your house and around your children.

I went to counseling several times throughout my life, and I was able to get the help I needed. Please know that whatever you may be going through, you can get through it! You have to learn how to love yourself. You have to learn how to forgive yourself and others. And you have to find someone you can confide in to help you along the way.

The following critical information is adapted from the Web site of the organization Stop It Now! Please visit www.StopItNow.org for more information.

Child sexual abuse is so often hidden, the statistics vary widely. The research that has been done shows that it's widespread and has a devastating impact on families and communities. As many as one in three girls and one in seven boys will be sexually abused at some point in their childhood. (Briere, J., Eliot, D.M. Prevalence and Psychological Sequence of Self-Reported Childhood Physical and Sexual Abuse in General Population: Child Abuse and Neglect, 2003, 27 10.)

- In as many as 93 percent of child sexual cases, the child knows the person who commits the abuse.
- Studies show that treatment for people who sexually abuse children can reduce the likelihood that they will reoffend.
- Up to 50 percent of those who sexually abuse children are under the age of eighteen.
- Eighty-eight percent of cases of sexual abuse are never reported to the authorities.
- The most effective prevention takes place before there's a child victim to heal or an offender to punish.
- Child sexual abuse happens in all racial, ethnic, religious, and age groups, and at all socio-economic levels.

Since children are abused in homes across the country (remember, as many as one in three girls are sexually abused), all adults need to learn what makes children vulnerable, how to recognize warning signs of those who may be sexually abusing children, and what to do if sexual abuse is suspected.

Discovering that a convicted sex offender is living in your neighborhood can stir a range of feelings—fear, anger, lack of safety, loss of control. Yet, how many child predators live in your neighborhood and have *not* been discovered—and are not being monitored? Knowing what to do if sexual abuse is suspected can make all the difference for the children around you, for your family, and for your confidence in handling a situation. The U.S. Department of Justice – National Sex Offender Public Website (NSOPW) is an unprecedented public safety resource that provides the public with access to sex offender data nationwide. NSOPW is a partnership between the U.S. Department of Justice and state, territorial, and tribal governments, working together for the safety of adults and children. For more information, visit http://www.nsopw.gov. (Adapted from Stop It Now! – Together We Can Prevent the Sexual Abuse of Children, http://www.stopitnow.org.)

REFERENCES

Amburn, E. (2012). Joe Louis Clark. *Senior Times, 13(9), 22-26.* Reprinted with permission from Tower Publications, SeniorTimesMagazine.com.

Briere, J., Eliot, D.M. Prevalence and Psychological Sequence of Self-Reported Childhood Physical and Sexual Abuse in General Population: Child Abuse and Neglect, 2003, 27 10.

Clark, J. & Picard, J. (1989). Laying down the law: Clark's strategy for saving our schools. Washington, DC: Regnery Gateway.

Eastside Yearbook, (1982). *Mirror (56).* Walsworth Publishing Company: Marceline, Missouri.

Eastside Yearbook, (1983). *Mirror (57).* Walsworth Publishing Company: Marceline, Missouri.

Eastside Yearbook, (1984). *Mirror (58).* Walsworth Publishing Company: Marceline, Missouri.

Eastside Yearbook, (1985). *Mirror (56).* Walsworth Publishing Company: Marceline, Missouri.

Eastside Yearbook, (1986). *Mirror - The story behind the ghosts or the ghosts behind the story (60).* Walsworth Publishing Company: Marceline, Missouri.

Eastside Yearbook, (1987). *Mirror (61).* Walsworth Publishing Company: Marceline, Missouri.

Eastside Yearbook, (1988). *Mirror (62).* Walsworth Publishing Company: Marceline, Missouri.

Eastside Yearbook, (1989). *Mirror (63).* Walsworth Publishing Company: Marceline, Missouri.

Miller, Olandha Pinky, "A Phenomenological Case Study of a Principal Leadership: The Influence of Mr. Clark's Leadership on Students, Teachers and Administrators at Eastside High School." Dissertation, Georgia State University, 2011. http://scholarworks.gsu.edu/eps_diss/85

Wilson, Octavia – Email – Wilsonoctavia33@yahoo.com http://www.nsopw.gov. http://www.stopitnow.org

ABOUT THE AUTHOR

Dr. Pinky Miller, a native of Paterson, New Jersey, was educated through the public school system, attending Public School Number 24 and the famed Paterson Eastside High School. Eastside was depicted in the 1989 movie *Lean on Me*, in which Morgan Freeman portrayed the controversial principal Dr. Joe Clark.

Dr. Miller received her Bachelor of Arts degree in Communication Studies, and her Master of Arts degree in Counseling and School Guidance, from Montclair State University. In 2011, she received her Doctor of Philosophy degree from Georgia State University.

Dr. Pinky Miller is a dynamic and compelling motivational speaker, and executive producer of the forthcoming documentary *Know Our Story*, which chronicles the failures and accomplishments of Dr. Clark's students and the real-life legacy of the bullhorn and the baseball bat.

Dr. Miller has more than eighteen years of experience working in higher education and has held positions as Hall Director/Academic Advisor, Area Coordinator, Assistant/Director of Residence Life and Housing, Assistant Dean of Students, and Vice President of Student Affairs. Dr. Miller loves working with college students, assisting them in times of crises, and helping guide them toward becoming successful citizens. She has been recognized for her ability to organize and motivate people to achieve their goals. Dr. Miller is a proud member of Alpha Kappa Alpha Sorority, Inc.

Dr. Miller is married to fellow Eastside alumnus Mr. Daryl L. Miller; they have five children together.

Life after Lean on Me can be found at www.Know-Our-Story.com as well as Amazon.com, Kindle, and other fine booksellers.

Made in the USA
San Bernardino, CA
08 August 2016